TACTICS
MADE
SIMPLE

Dedicated to my Dad,
the bravest man I know.

TACTICS MADE SIMPLE

Sailboat racing tactics explained simply

Jon Emmett

FERNHURST
BOOKS

First published in 2019 and reprinted in 2021, 2023 & 2024 by Fernhurst Books Limited
Copyright © 2019 Fernhurst Books Limited

The Windmill, Mill Lane, Harbury, Leamington Spa, Warwickshire. CV33 9HP, UK
Tel: +44 (0) 1926 337488 | www.fernhurstbooks.com

A catalogue record for this book is available from the British Library
ISBN 978-1-912177-25-7

Front cover photograph © Richard Langdon / Sailing Energy
Back cover photograph & p5, 11: Tim Hore © Fernhurst Books
Other photographs ©:
Jon Emmett: p41
Tom Gruitt: p51
Jeremy Atkins: p66, 75, 87

Designed & illustrated by Daniel Stephen
Printed in Malta by Melita

JON EMMETT

GOLD MEDAL WINNING COACH & WORLD CHAMPION SAILOR

Jon Emmett is a professional sailing coach who coached Lijia Xu to win the gold medal in the Laser Radial Class at the London 2012 Olympics. He coached Lijia again for the 2016 Rio Olympics and has since coached sailors from the United Kingdom, Israel, Malaysia, Finland and Argentina aiming for the Olympics. He is also the Training Officer for the UK Laser Class Association.

As well as coaching, Jon is a very successful and regular competitor, with successes including:

Byte C II Class
- World Champion
- European Champion

ILCA 6 / Laser Radial Class
- Masters World Champion (7 times)
- Masters European Champion (8 times)
- UK National Champion (9 times)
- UK National Ranking Series Winner (over 10 times)
- UK Inland Nationals Champion (over 10 times)

Jon is also author of Fernhurst Books' *Coach Yourself to Win*, *Be Your Own Sailing Coach* (ebook only), *Be Your Own Tactics Coach* (ebook only) and *Training to Win*. Jon is also co-author of *The ILCA Book*

www.jonemmettsailing.co.uk

CONTENTS

FOREWORD

To win sailboat races you need to be able to sail the boat fast.

To consistently win races and win regattas you need to sail smart and fast, making the right decisions to sail the best course. If you are not the fastest boat you are still able to win races and regattas by managing risk and sailing smart. This is where good tactics come in.

Boatspeed comes down to hours of on the water training and tuning. Feel is developed over time and can be very different from boat to boat – there are few shortcuts to hours practising on the water.

Tactics are quite different and may be learnt and fast tracked more easily by thinking about each leg of the course and different situations from the comfort of your own home!

Jon Emmett's new book, *Tactics Made Simple*, is a great tool to help fast track learning.

Jon is an extremely talented coach with a great passion for the sport. He has worked closely with several international teams over the years whose first language was not always English. In the book he explains each tactical situation very well with clear diagrams and limited text. A nice touch is the individual boats in each scenario being identified with names so that you can easily understand the situation.

Each chapter takes you around the race course, from before you get on the water (which is often overlooked), through to the pre-start, start, different legs and manoeuvres. Each section contains detailed advice for the beginner, intermediate and advanced sailor so you can look at the relevant level, and how to progress to the next.

Jon's passion and experience not only as a coach but also a great sailor (who still competes and wins international regattas) gives him a unique position to breakdown and explain complex tactical situations in an easily understandable format.

This book is a must for any sailor who wants to improve their tactical skills. With reading, understanding and practice you will become a better sailor and tactician.

Sail smart, sail fast, good luck!

Paul Goodison
Olympic gold medallist (Laser), 6 x World Champion (International Moth x 3, Laser, Melges 20, Melges 32), winner of the 2017 Star Sailors League Finals

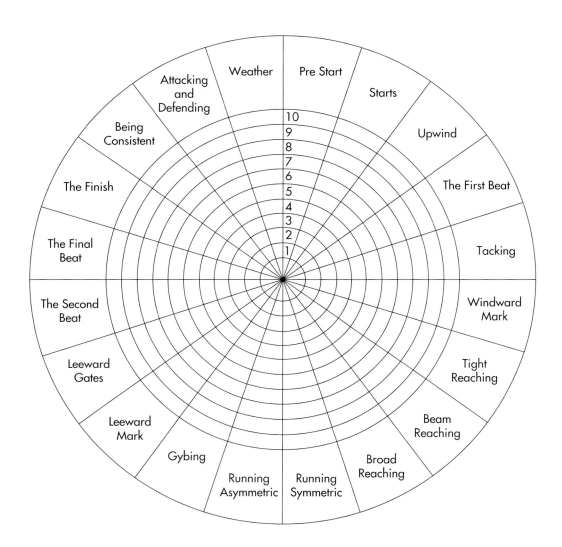

Performance dartboard

Introduction

Welcome to *Tactics Made Simple*. As with my other books (*Coach Yourself to Win* and *Training to Win*), the aim is to produce a book that is very user friendly, so you really can get the most out of it by putting in the minimum of effort and just reading the sections you need to.

To make the book even more accessible each chapter has been divided into three sections which are colour coded as follows:

- Beginner   ORANGE
- Intermediate   **GREEN**
- Advanced   **BLUE**

This makes it easy for people new to racing to get the basic concepts, whilst more advanced racers can go straight to the information they need without having to wade through lots of stuff they are already very familiar with.

Top class sailing is all about that extra final percent, but you need to get the basics right as well. You can race extremely well by just getting the 'big' things right (always sailing the right way up the beat, etc.) before you worry about 'smaller' things (which side to position yourself to your main opposition). It is definitely worth mentioning that you should not allow the smaller things (covering the opposition) to override the bigger issue (which way to go up the beat) or both you and your closest opposition could end up having a bad result (although, in some cases, this 'may' be what you want). Just remember what is going on, and don't forget the basics.

Just like improving any aspect of your sailing, you need to be focused. Before delving into the book, I would suggest that you fill out the dartboard opposite, as you did for *Coach Yourself to Win*, to make sure you are working on the areas that will help you improve the most. You can then go and practise these tactics or at least be more aware of them when you train or just during your club race.

To make it easy to remember, the boat's 'surname' has been designed to give an indication as to how they are sailing. For example: Finlay Footing likes to sail the boat fast and free and you may be able to identify yourself or someone you race against as like him. This will explain what your best option is and how to deal with him or her. Please note the names represent the helm / tactician and are therefore male and female (although all boats are, of course, female).

There is a full index of all the characters in the back of the book. Each boat has its own distinct colour.

I hope you enjoy improving your tactics.

CHAPTER 1

Pre-Start

BASIC PREPARATIONS (BEGINNER)

Before you even decide to enter the race / regatta, make sure you are properly prepared. How long does it take to the venue? (Giving you enough rest.) Have you sorted out good accommodation? When do you need to enter? (Many regattas implement a surcharge if you enter late, so make your mind up!) Is your boat race-ready and do you have all the spares you need?

Read the sailing instructions so you know the course you are racing, where it is and when; and don't forget to check the official notice board for changes to the SIs (sailing instructions) as it is not uncommon for amendments to be made. World Championships have been won and lost when people didn't notice a change of start time.

Races can be decided before the warning signal is even blown. Establish what the most important tactic(s) will be for the day. Get the big things sorted (like not over-standing the layline with strong current under you) before you worry about the little things (a small amount of dirty air).

You need to break things down so, first of all, consider the variables that will affect the course you would sail in the absence of other boats.

Current

A strong favourable current (or less adverse current) on one side of the course may be the most important factor, especially with slower moving boats. You can check the current by placing a 2/3 full bottle of liquid by a mark and seeing how far it moves in a minute. (Pick it up afterwards.)

If the wind is offshore, you can check the current on your sail out to the start line. Launch early to give yourself plenty of time.

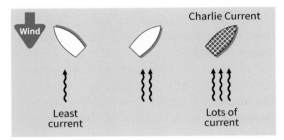

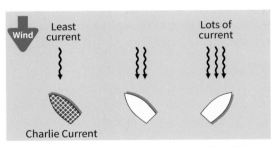

Charlie Current is always keen to maximise his tidal advantage compared to other boats

Windshifts / Bends

If there is a big shift, getting to it first can make a real difference. You may be expecting this windshift because of a weather forecast or, if the wind is stable, you may see the shift affecting boats further to windward or there may be a wind bend due to the shore line.

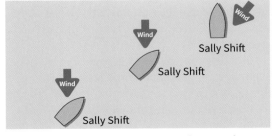

Sally Shift is always keen to maximise the gain of an expected big shift

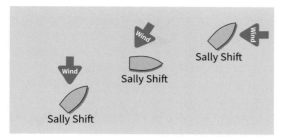

Sally Shift also likes to maximise the gain from an expected wind bend

Get out on the race course early – the precise placement of the race course will affect your tactics. (The exact position of the racing area should be given in the Sailing Instructions.) If there is an oscillating breeze, try to get in tune with it (work out the frequency and duration). If not just practise your tacking!!

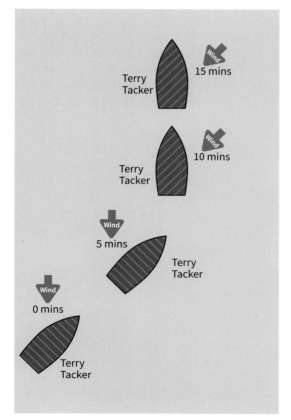

Terry Tacker likes to tack in a shifting breeze

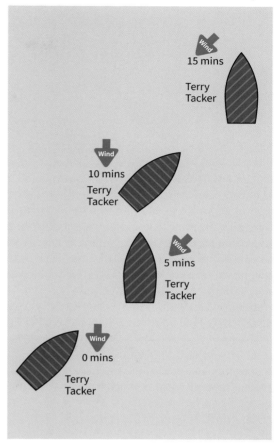

Terry Tacker also likes to gain by tacking in an oscillating breeze

Wind Speed / Pressure

With a big difference in wind speed, the windier side of the course may be heavily favoured, especially with boats which plane upwind.

More wind makes the water look darker so, when an area of the water is dark, there is more wind there. Where there are more white horses there is also more wind than in the flatter areas (assuming no current difference).

In light winds (under 7 knots) even a small difference in wind speed (say 4-6 knots) can make a big difference in boatspeed.

If the breeze is offshore, you can probably work out which is the windiest part of the race course on the way to the start line.

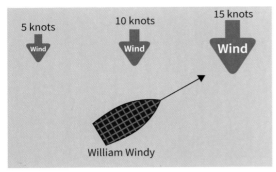

William Windy is always off to the windiest part of the race course to help his boat go as fast as possible

Finally, in terms of basic preparation, don't forget good boatwork is essential. To look at the more technical side (before you even hit the water) see chapter 12 in *Coach Yourself to Win* (Preparation & Note Taking).

SPOTTING THE CHANGES (INTERMEDIATE)

Wind awareness is key (especially in light winds). Ensure that you pay careful attention to changes in wind strength (darker or lighter patches on the

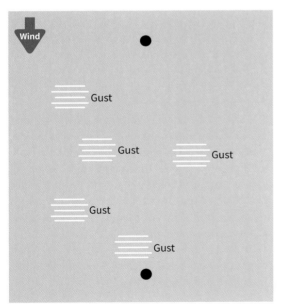

There would appear to be more wind on the left-hand side of the race course

water for stronger / lighter areas of wind) and shifts (which are often the key reason for tacking (see Chapters 3: Upwind and 4: The First Beat). By having a good look before the start, you should know what to expect (but you will still need to keep your head out of the boat).

You can also expect changes in current. Now obviously you don't have time to drop a tide stick in during a race, but you can make observations such as how the current is affecting you (using transits) and examining any buoys that you pass. The buoys will appear to be travelling towards the current with a small amount of slack water behind the buoy (pointing the way the current is going). The faster the buoys appear to be going (the more bow waves at the front and the greater the slack water behind), the stronger the current. Hence you can see if the current is increasing or decreasing and if there is any change in direction.

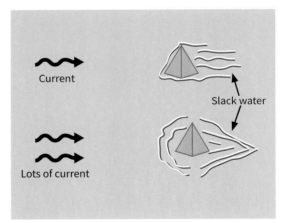

The effect of current on a buoy

There may also be expected changes in the wind direction. For example, if there is a sea breeze (in the northern hemisphere) you would expect the mean wind direction to go to the right (although the wind can still be shifty with a sea breeze). So, make sure you know what compass heading a header is and what a lift is. If you are sailing at 180° in the morning, for example, this might be a lift, while in the afternoon, if you are sailing at 180°, this could now be a header.

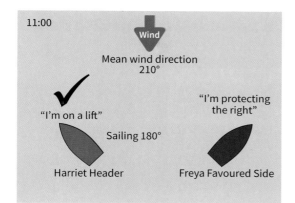

In the morning, Harriet Header is on a lift sailing at 180°

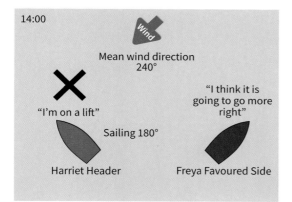

But in the afternoon, Harriet Header's 180° is no longer a lift

THOSE FINAL FEW MINUTES (ADVANCED)

Those final few minutes just before the start are absolutely crucial. In fact, in some ways, the results of the race can be decided before it has even begun! This is not the time to be simply reaching around enjoying the breeze…

So, the most important thing is to focus. Time often has a variable quality. While you are waiting for the race committee to start the sequence, time may seem to drag, but the last minute can absolutely fly by and you suddenly find yourself over or further behind the line than you hoped.

Remember that sailing is a non-contact sport! And the racing rules start from the preparatory signal (the rules still apply but there is no penalty

for breaking them – unless there is damage which would mean you have to retire from the race). However, you must not interfere with a boat who is already racing. You are technically racing when the preparatory signal has gone. You should be awake from the warning signal, looking for information about the race, but at the preparatory signal you should be 100% focused – after all you are now racing!

The rules state that, at the preparatory signal, your boat should be afloat (I know a few club racers who tend to launch at the preparatory signal). You want to check the starting penalty as this will affect how you approach the start. The most commonly used options are:

 P flag: No penalty: you simply need to dip back behind the line after the start if you were over at the starting signal otherwise you would be scored OCS.

 I flag: you are disqualified if you are over with a minute or less to go unless you return to the pre-start side of the course going around the ends of the line.

 Z flag: you have 20% of the number of boats in the fleet added to your score if you are over the start line with a minute or less to go (the % may vary depending upon the sailing instructions).

 U flag: you are disqualified if you are over the start line with a minute or less to go for this start, but you can take part in subsequent starts if the start is re-run.

 Black flag: you are disqualified if you are over the start line with a minute or less to go for this and subsequent starts of that race.

Remember whether you get a good start or not is only clear about 10 seconds after the start. So, keep going. That boat which is about to roll / leebow you may hit a wave and stop, allowing you to break through.

Your build up to the start of the first race of the day (for a race of around an hour) should be something like this:

Time to start	Focus
60 minutes*	Check and double check your boat and launch, checking the conditions on your way out. Register with the committee boat if needed (in some regattas you have to show your sail number on entering the racing area).
50 minutes	Do a practice beat. You don't have to do the whole thing, but you need to be comfortable that you know which way you want to go.
30 minutes	Downwind boat handling. Practise a kite hoist and gybe and then pack the kite on the correct side for the first hoist in the race.
20 minutes	Double check the rig set up. Are you expecting the wind to drop or increase? Is the beat still the same as it was 30 minutes ago? If not, what is changing?
10 minutes	Check out the start line and keep checking. Depending upon the regatta the warning signal may go now.
5 minutes	Now into starting sequence – so focus!

In the final minute, it is crucial that you are in the correct area of the line as shown in the diagram below.

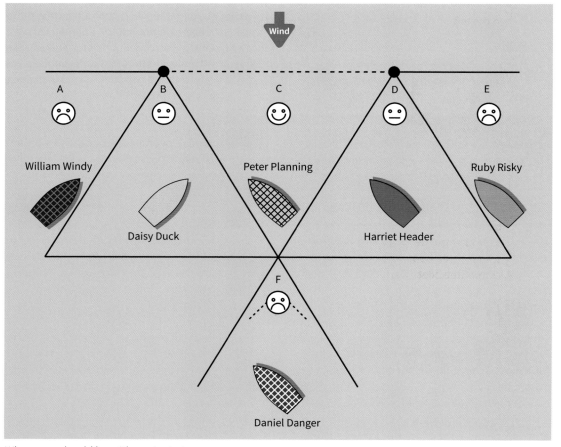

Where you should be with a minute to go

Area	Reason	Happy?	Options
A	William Windy was on the left side of the course then the wind died, and he could not get back to the starting area.	Sad	Not only does he have to duck any starboard tackers, he must also keep clear of the leeward boats in B as he is windward boat.
B	Daisy Duck has left coming into the starting area a bit late, but all is not lost.	Not happy	She should be able to duck a few boats and get to the line. She just has to pray a gap opens up!
C	Peter Planning is in the triangle that means he can definitely cross the line. If right was favoured, he would be further to the right; if left was favoured, he would be further to the left.	Happy	Peter Planning can look for a gap and start where he wants.
D	Harriet Header got the wind wrong. She thought she was on the layline to the start line, but she was above it.	Not happy	If she can see a gap further down the line she should get in it as soon as possible. Otherwise she has to stay up and clear of the leeward boats in C, hoping a gap opens up, or stay where she is and tack for clear air as soon as the boats in C have started.
E	Ruby Risky thought a gap was going to open up by the committee boat, but it didn't. There is now a whole queue of boats in the waiting area hoping to start by the committee boat.	Sad	If there is a gap, go for it. Otherwise stay clear and hope the boats are drifting fast. She will have to wait for those boats in C and D to start. She can then go behind them and tack to the right, hoping not too many people have done this already.
F	Daniel Danger was way too late getting out to the starting area and will probably miss the start.	Very sad (crying his eyes out)	Hope for a general recall!!!

CHAPTER 2

Starts

WHERE TO START (BEGINNER)

Line Bias

In the absence of other factors, you would want to start next to the end of the line which was the most upwind, not necessarily that which was closest to the first mark (because boats cannot sail straight into the wind).

You must continually check the bias of the line as it can change. If the line bias is two boat lengths, that equals three boat lengths' sailing (as we sail at approximately 45 degree angle to the wind!). Therefore, do not stray too far away from what you consider to be the favoured end with ten minutes to go.

Finish Line Bias

If you are finishing going upwind through the start line, then the favoured end of the finish line is the opposite end to the favoured end of the start line, assuming nothing has changed during the course of the race.

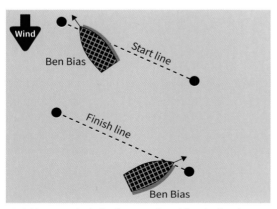

Finishing upwind, the favoured end for the finish is the opposite to the favoured end for the start

But if you are finishing going downwind through the start line, then the favoured end of the start is the same as the finish.

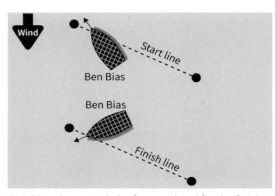

Finishing downwind, the favoured end for the finish is the same as the favoured end for the start

Course Bias

However, line bias isn't the only factor when considering which end to start. From your pre-start strategy, you may have decided that you must go one way upwind. This means that you may choose to start away from the most upwind end of the line if it makes it easier to go where you want.

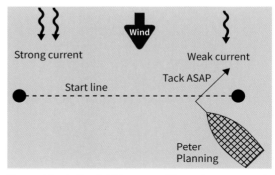

Course bias to the right because of less adverse current

Course bias comes in many forms. The course might be biased (favoured) one side due to the strength of the current or wind, or an expected or persistent windshift. You would really worry if the course were offset if it was very small and / or you were likely to end up over the laylines because it doesn't matter if you spend more time on one tack, just what your VMG to the next mark is.

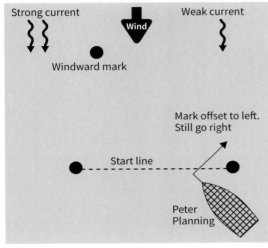

Although the windward mark is offset to the left, the course bias is still to the right because of less adverse current

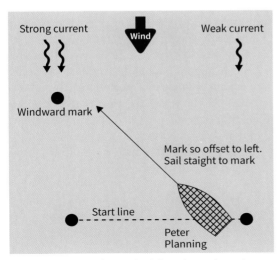

With the mark so offset to the left, sail straight to the mark despite the adverse current

Transits

It is usually easier to judge your position on the line nearer an end. Any part of the boat can be over: it is simply the part which is most upwind. In other words if you are in the middle of the boat on the line, then you are half a boat length over…

Starting in the middle of the line (more than 25% from either end) it is harder to judge where the line is (as you are further from the ends). Here a good transit is essential to avoid the mid line sag which could be several boat lengths on a long line.

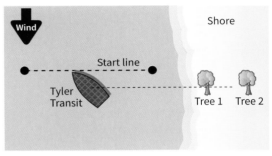

Tyler Transit has a transit showing when he is on the line

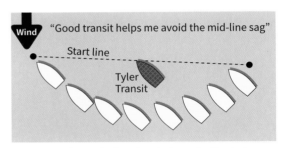

Having good transits for when he is on the line helps Tyler Transit avoid the mid-line sag

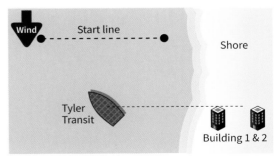

Tyler Transit also has a transit showing when he is behind the line

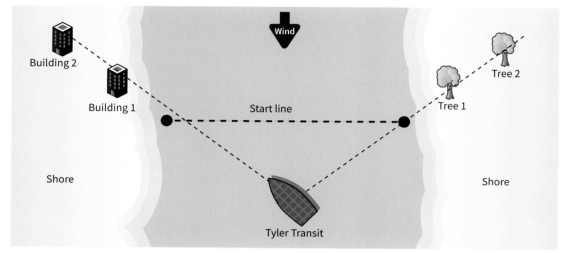

Tyler Transit also has transits showing when he is on the layline for each end of the line

Timing

Ensure that you have accurate timing: check this at the 5-, 4- and 1-minute signals.

Also check out how long it takes you to get up to full speed. Remember the wind and waves at start time can be confused, making it harder to accelerate. Talk everything through with the people you sail with and have a few dummy runs.

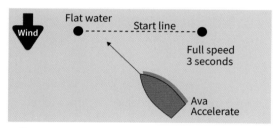

In flat water, Ava Accelerate takes 3 seconds to get to full speed

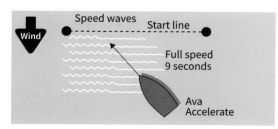

In big waves, Ava Accelerate takes 9 seconds to get to full speed

BIG FLEET STARTS (INTERMEDIATE)

Although many international fleets will sail round robins or have restricted entries, meaning fleet numbers are smaller, there are still plenty of national regattas which have long start lines (perhaps taking five minutes to sail down). So, it is well worth getting the tactics right, because starting in big fleets is one of the most difficult skills to master as it is hard to practise (there are a limited number of big fleet starts for each class, each year).

Improving your starting in big fleets is one of the best ways to improve your overall results. If you can come off the line in the first ten boats then you are already in a secure position, on the 'escalator' to the windward mark. Meanwhile the rest of the boats are:

- Either sitting in dirty air and going slower
- Or sailing on the 'wrong' (heading) tack and sailing more distance

They are effectively stepping down the 'escalator' because they are not making maximum progress to the next mark (as if they had just taken a step backwards on the escalator).

The following diagrams show some ways to get good big fleet start.

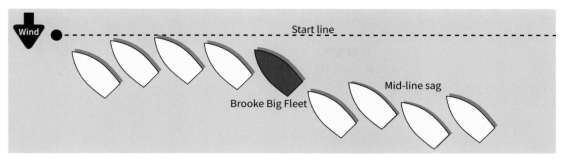

Port-end Brooke wants to go right: he is not over the line and can easily tack

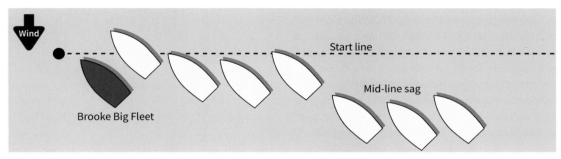

Port-end Brooke wants to go left: he is not over the line and can easily get left

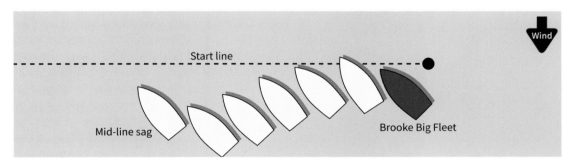

Starboard-end Brooke wants to go right: he is not over the line and can easily tack

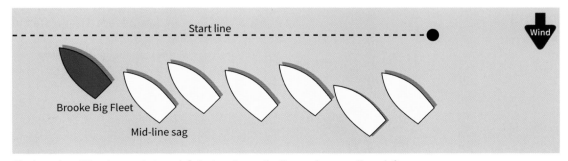

Starboard-end Brooke wants to go left: he is not over the line and can easily go left

Winning the end can be very important. For a port end favoured line, the port tack approach can work very well to control the fleet.

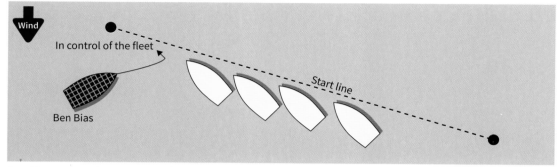

Ben Bias approaches on port tack and is in control of the fleet

For a starboard favoured line, we need to position ourselves up drift of the favoured end so, as we gradually drift down the line, we end up in the perfect place at start time. After all, life is all about being in the right place at the right time. If the starboard end is a large committee boat you may wish to start a boat length or two away from it, if it is producing a large wind shadow.

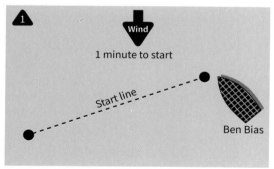

With 1 minute to the start, Ben Bias is up-drift of the favoured starboard end

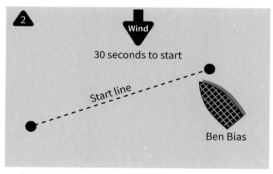

With 30 seconds to go, Ben Bias has drifted slightly

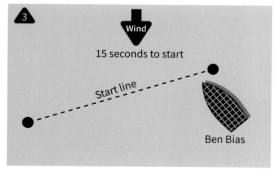

With 15 seconds to go, Ben Bias is holding a good position

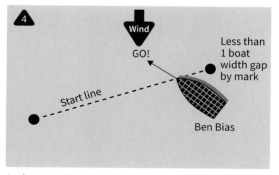

At the start, Ben Bias has less than one boat width gap by the mark and can go – he has won the end

For an even line and perhaps one where you are not sure which way you want to go (or it is a shifty day and you just want to keep your options open) start towards the middle of the line. Then move down the line either coming from behind and then luffing up into a gap or sailing down on port and tacking under someone with a good gap.

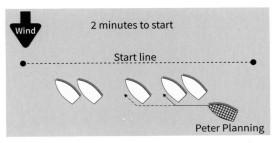

With 2 minutes to go, Peter Planning sails down the line and luffs into a gap

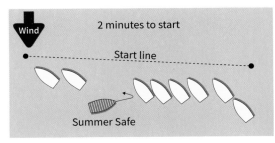

With 2 minutes to go, Summer Safe approaches on port and tacks under someone with a good gap

KNOWING YOUR RIGHTS (ADVANCED)

Knowing your rights at start time is absolutely crucial. It is not simply he (or she) who shouts loudest who has right of way (and there are few places on the race course which have as much shouting as the start line). I still hear people shouting "mast abeam", a term which has not been in the rules for many, many years!

In a perfect world you would simply find your space and, at the appropriate time, accelerate like Ava Accelerate did on p20. However, this is not always possible, so we may end up having to tack in like Ben Bias (p22) or slot in from behind like Peter Planning above.

Before the start, there is no proper course and so you can luff up to head to wind as long as you give the other boats room to keep clear. After the start, if you did not approach from behind (Ben Bias tacked in) you may still luff up to head to wind as long as the other boats can keep clear but, if you approached from behind (like Peter Planning – opposite) you cannot sail above your proper course if it affects other boats. This is why it is good to tack underneath someone rather than come in from behind – it gives you more options.

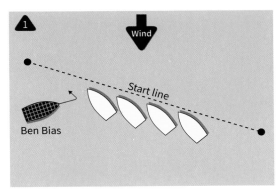

Ben Bias tacked in

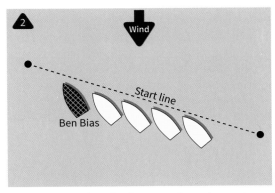

Ben Bias says: "The other boats can keep clear, so I may luff as hard as I like"

If, however, you are looking to start at the starboard end you will most likely have boats to leeward of you. You must keep clear of these. However, they must give you room to keep clear. (They cannot simply sail in about 1 cm from your boat and expect you to be able to keep clear.)

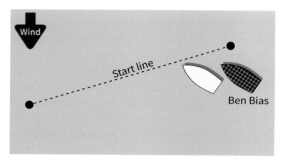

If he is luffed, Ben Bias can keep clear, and must

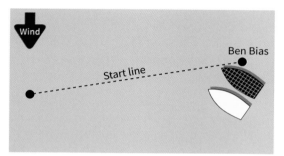

In this position, if he is luffed, Ben Bias cannot keep clear, so he cannot be luffed

This is a key idea where the right of way boat must give the give way boat room to keep clear. Here Peter Planning has lined up for a port flyer: he is keeping clear of Sophie Starboard who has to hold her course, as if she changed her course Peter Planning would not be able to keep clear.

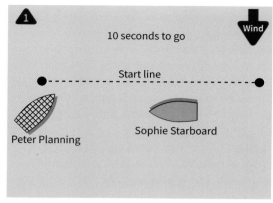

Sophie Starboard is the right of way boat

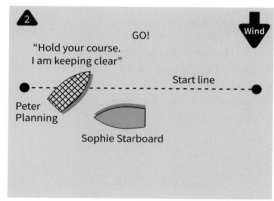

Peter Planning is keeping clear and Sophie Starboard cannot head up to her proper course to prevent him keeping clear

BASIC UPWIND SAILING (BEGINNER)

When you are sailing upwind your goal is to minimise the amount of time it takes you to get to the windward mark. It is not to maximise your speed (you could reach around all day and make no progress upwind), nor is it to point as close as possible to the wind (as you will end up going very slowly). Nevertheless, it is possible to sail a range of angles and still make equally good progress upwind (velocity made good: VMG, that is speed in the desired direction) as demonstrated by Finlay Footing and Poppy Pinching.

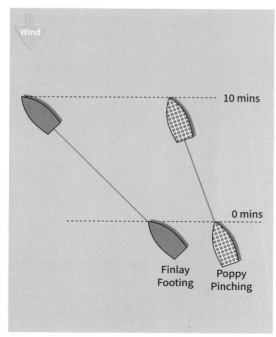

Finlay Footing and Poppy Pinching are sailing at different angles but have the same VMG because they travel the same distance upwind in the same time

However, in terms of ease of getting to the windward mark, somewhere in between is usually better as it is easier to sail to. The problem with Finlay Footing is that you can easily lose height for no extra speed (ending up sailing lower but at the same speed) and the problem with Poppy Pinching is that you can easily lose speed trying to stay high. Being in the middle you are less likely to make an error as you can sail slightly higher or lower and still maintain maximum VMG. It will also probably be easier to hold your lane as this is likely to be the angle most other boats are sailing at.

But there are times when footing is very good: to get across to one side of the race course, perhaps to roll over another boat (get to windward and give them dirty air) or to get to a favoured side of the course: for example, out of bad current, into stronger wind or to be the first person into the new shift.

Likewise pinching has its place: if you want to stay away from one side of the course (it is a shifty day and you want to stay in the middle of the course) or perhaps to stay out of adverse tide or to leebow another boat.

So, for example, if you have been on a starboard lift for a long time, you may tend to pinch on starboard tack so as not to get too far away from the centre of the course and then, as soon as the port lift comes in, foot on port tack to get back over to the centre of the course as quickly as possible.

This also means that you cross the other boats as soon as possible (you have not secured any gain to windward unless you are directly to windward of your rivals because, if the wind shifts again towards the other boats, they gain on you – so, if the wind went to the right, the boats on the right would gain).

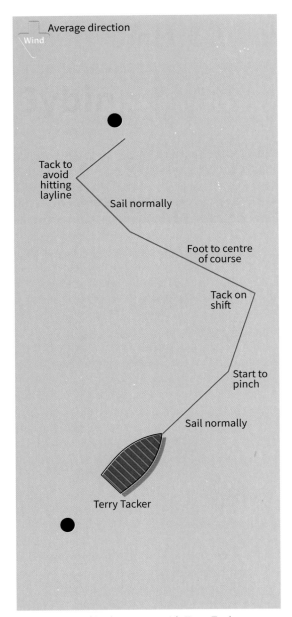

Staying central in the course with Terry Tacker

Whether you pinch, or foot, may be related to the weight of the crew (it is easier for heavier crews to foot, especially in strong winds, and it is easier for light crews to pinch, especially in light winds) or to the rig set up. For more information see chapter 4 in *Coach Yourself to Win* (Upwind Boatspeed).

DEALING WITH THE CONDITIONS (INTERMEDIATE)

What is the wind like today? Is it steady in speed and direction, or is it constantly changing?

In light winds, avoid too much leeward heel. Leeward heel may make it feel as if you have more power, but it will increase the drag. Instead move your weight forward to decrease drag. This will also give you more feel on the rudder, helping you to steer more accurately for changes in wind speed and direction. Remember, in really light winds, pressure is king as it will not only help you to go faster but you will also point higher (as your sails and foils become more efficient).

In medium winds you can now get the boat up to full speed. The best plan is usually to get the boat up to full speed first and then you can aim for pointing (turning additional power into height). If you try to pinch first, you risk stalling the sails and foils meaning that it will take longer to get to maximum VMG. If your boat planes to windward then, in theory, there is no maximum VMG!!!

In strong winds you are really looking to depower the rig (see chapter 4 in *Coach Yourself to Win* – Upwind Boatspeed – for explanations on flattening sails, raking the mast and inducing leech twist). Sailing in strong winds is difficult, so you need to make it as easy as possible. Hike / trapeze as hard as you can consistently and keep the steering smooth. Keep the boat completely flat and make sure you use good equipment (old sails are likely to be stretched, old masts will have poorer gust response, etc.).

In gusty conditions the wind will usually be very unstable (there is a lot of mixing with the stronger winds coming down) or shifty (where they are affected by coming over a land mass, especially hills, mountains, etc.).

Gusts are usually clearly visible on the water, but they come in different shapes and sizes: sometimes long thin streaks where the wind has funnelled between buildings, and sometimes large cat paws where the wind has come down from above and is spreading out.

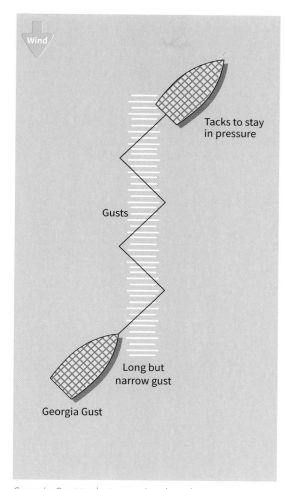

Georgia Gust tacks to stay in a long but narrow gust

If you are in a boat which planes upwind, gusts can be especially useful as there will be a clear speed advantage if you can maximise your time spent in stronger winds. You just need to weigh up whether it is worth sailing more distance for the extra speed you get if you get to the gust. The key is to get your head out of the boat and see if there is a pattern, perhaps more gusts on one side of the course.

When going upwind you will, of course, have a greater frequency of gusts as you are sailing towards the wind. You need to set your boat up to achieve the highest average speed. Depending upon the frequency of the gusts, this means being underpowered in the lulls, perfectly set up for the mean wind and slightly overpowered in the gusts. However, the more frequent the gusts, the closer your rig will be optimised for them.

The harder the conditions (big slamming gusts) the more you need to make your boat easy to sail (perhaps playing the sheet more or sailing with a softer leech) as you can lose a great deal if the boat stalls, and even more if you end up going for a swim.

The bigger the area of the gust (with more dark water with a bigger gust), the longer it will last, and the faster it approaches the greater the wind speed. Depending upon where the gust comes from it may also affect the wind direction.

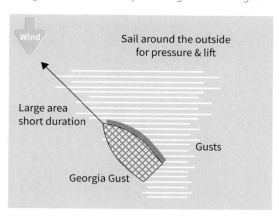

Georgia Gust sails around the outside of a fat wide gust for pressure and lift

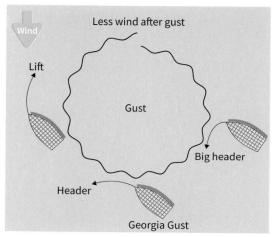

The gust's effect on Georgia depends on which direction the gusts are approaching

27

For a boat on starboard tack:

Gust from	Actions
Ahead	Header
The right	Lift
The left	Big header

On port it would be the opposite effect to starboard.

WHEN TO TACK (ADVANCED)

Hopefully most of the time the option when to tack will be your decision, not forced on you by another boat or because you have unintentionally sailed to the layline. Let us go through a few examples.

Before the start you got out on the water nice and early and noticed that the wind which is coming from the north (of a south facing shore) is shifting a lot as the course is not far from the shore line. The range is between 350° and 10° (with 0° being the average). So which tack should you be on?

Terry Tacker is always on starboard in 10°, port in 350° and on the tack which takes him towards the centre of the race course in 0°.

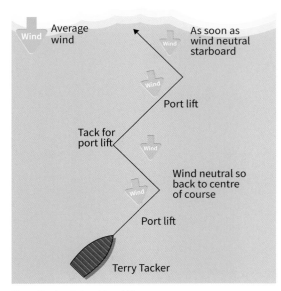

Terry Tacker takes the shifts

Now (maybe after several general recalls and not being able to get the race away) the race officer moves the race course 2 miles offshore. Here the wind is between 355° and 5° (compass bearing): a fairly regular oscillation. The key here is to take advantage of the big shift.

Sally Shift flips onto starboard as soon as the wind is 0° and increasing and back to port as soon as the wind is 0° (compass bearing) to make the most of the big shift.

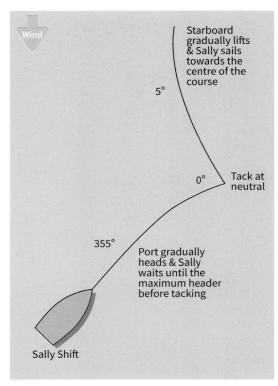

Sally Shift sails the wind bend

After the first race, which was sailed at low water (to give a large launching area), the tide changes. The direction of the current changes inshore first where the water is shallower. It is now important to play the current.

If the current is across the race course, it gives an effective shift, meaning that it pays to start down current. However, be careful that you can cross the start line!

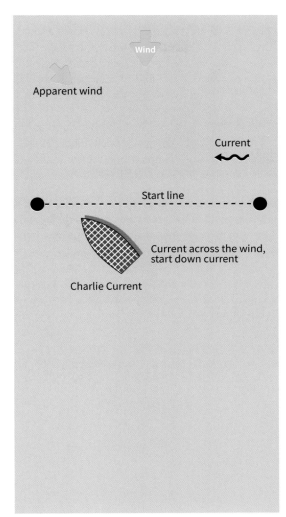

Charlie Current plays the cross current to his advantage

If the current is lined up with the wind, you need to be heading for the most favourable current or the least adverse current, but be careful as the current will affect the laylines, and you don't want to over-stand the mark. You don't want to come out of the favourable current too soon (having to do two extra tacks in some boats can be disastrous).

The favourable current squeezes the laylines together (making them narrower and easier to accidently over-stand) whereas adverse current stretches the laylines (making them wider and easier to accidently under-stand).

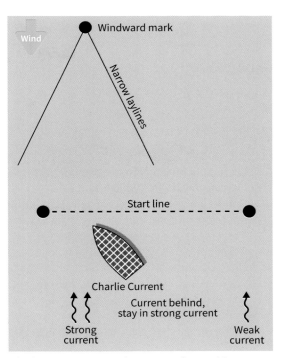

Charlie Current stays in the stronger favourable current, but is aware of narrow laylines

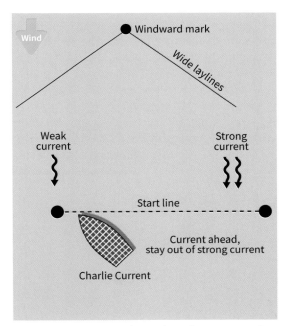

Charlie Current stays in the weaker adverse current, but is aware of wider laylines

The next day the wind changes direction so that it is now parallel to the land which is quite high, causing a wind bend. Sally Shift makes the most of this by sailing right into the bend before tacking whereas Terry Tacker loses out by tacking too early.

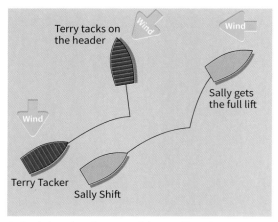

Sally Shift makes the most of the wind bend

With the wind dying, the course is now brought further inshore but away from the hill. There is now a large difference in pressure (northern hemisphere) with more wind offshore (it would be the opposite in the southern hemisphere).

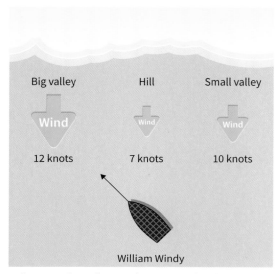

William Windy is off to get the most wind and win the race

You can easily predict which way the tide will run on the race course by using a tidal atlas (these will usually be available from the local chandlery, but it may be worth ringing ahead to make sure). However, you should always check the current by getting out on the course early because predictions are just that, predictions and, just like a weather forecast…, they can be wrong (the predictions are based on past data and do not take account of current conditions such as wind, pressure, etc.).

During the course of the day the current is gradually moving to the right and therefore you would expect to gain by going left. Just as you would if the wind was actually going left.

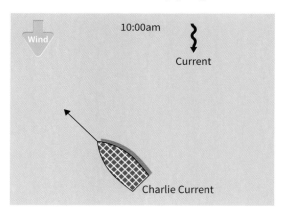

With the current in line with the wind, it doesn't affect tactics if the current is equal across the course

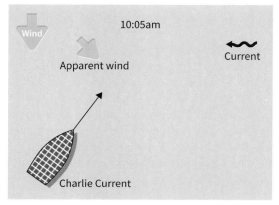

With the current moving from right to left, Charlie Current gets a lift on port because of the leebow effect

Often the effects of the current will be more noticeable on the beat than the run. The best way to tell if you are getting the current correct is to keep taking transits to see where you are going compared to the direction the boat is pointing (which may be a very different direction).

When sailing directly with or against the current there is no point pinching or footing unless by doing so it will keep you in less adverse current / get you into less adverse current sooner. As always you should be considering maximum velocity made good (VMG). (The same goes if the current is directly under you.)

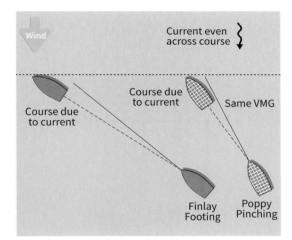

Don't unnecessarily foot or pinch in adverse current

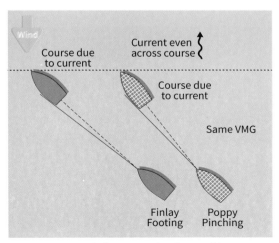

Don't unnecessarily foot or pinch in favourable current

Your final position in relation to the fleet depends on whether you think the wind is going right or left or is constant. Play it safe and try to put yourself in a position where you can take advantage of the next windshift. So, if the wind has shifted to the right, you are going left but able to tack as soon as it goes back to the left again.

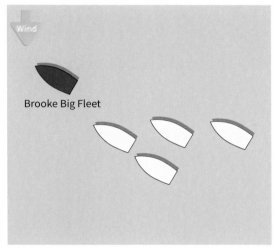

Brooke Big Fleet has positioned himself to the left because he thinks the wind is going to go left and, therefore, he will gain the most advantage from the shift

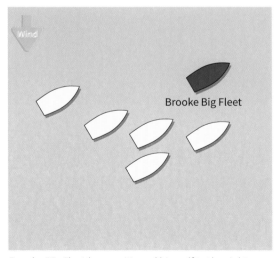

Brooke Big Fleet has positioned himself to the right because he thinks the wind is going to go right and, therefore, he will gain the most advantage from the shift

31

You would position yourself further across if you believe the change is definitely going to happen. For example, if you know the current is going to change (becoming stronger, weaker or change direction) and this will, therefore, affect the wind (stronger adverse current gives less wind, stronger favourable current gives more wind, cross current gives a windshift in the downtide direction).

So, looking at a cross current left to right, you know the wind is going to shift to the left, or cross current right to left you know the wind is going to shift to the right, so you would position yourself further to the favoured side like Brooke Big Fleet. Or perhaps you can just see what is happening to the fleet in front of you and want to take advantage of this.

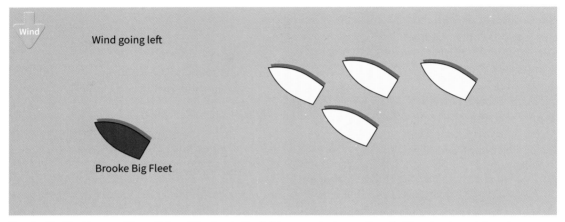

Brooke Big Fleet has positioned himself further to the left because he knows the wind is going to go left and, therefore, he will gain the most advantage from the shift

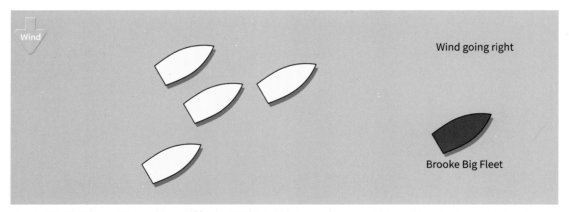

Brooke Big Fleet has positioned himself further to the right because he knows the wind is going to go right and, therefore, he will gain the most advantage from the shift

FIRST BEAT BASICS (BEGINNER)

Your position at the first mark is crucial. After this point it can be hard to make significant place changes. So, in a major championship, simply being in the top ten round the windward mark can make a real difference to your overall regatta performance. For one thing, the front of the fleet tend to fight less amongst themselves and just sail fast, pulling away from everyone else.

With most regattas having many races and few discards, being consistent is very important in order not to get too many high scores. See Chapter 18 (Being Consistent).

If you go all the way to one side of the course, then you risk not being able to take advantage of a shift later on because you may have to sail on a header to get to the mark, meaning that you sail more distance than your rivals.

To help you stay towards the centre of the course, or towards the centre of the favoured side of the course relative to other boats, you can alter your mode of sailing. If you are on the left of other boats and you are expecting the wind to go right, you want to foot like Finlay to consolidate your gain.

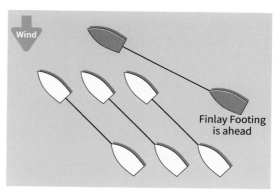

Finlay Footing consolidates his gain

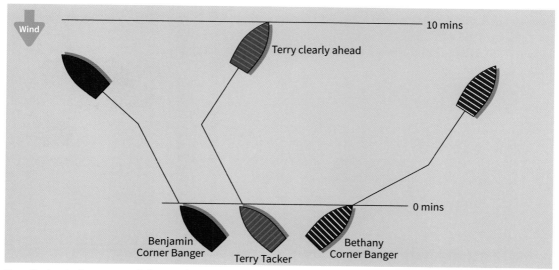

Terry Tacker tacks on every shift: everything else being equal, this is a safe bet

The class of boat makes a big difference to the way you sail. In a slow boat which turns without losing ground to windward, you would tack on even the smallest windshift (perhaps when sailing on a small inland lake surrounded by trees) as there is potential gain to be had for very little loss. However, with a faster boat which loses more speed when tacking (a twin trapeze catamaran for example), you would only tack when you are sure it is time to.

MEETING OTHER BOATS (INTERMEDIATE)

One of the things about the first beat is that the boats are much closer together and so there tends to be much more boat-to-boat interaction, which means that the opportunity for place changing is much higher. So, you need to make your decision rather than having it forced upon you. Try to think ahead, not only how you are going to get clean wind but also how you are going to keep it! The options are as follows:

1. Ducking Boats
Maybe you are on port for a reason (you want to get to the right-hand side of the course for more pressure or you think a bigger starboard lift is coming). To do a good duck make sure you pass as close to the rudder of the other boat as possible and then head up onto a close-hauled course, like Daisy Duck. You may even want to ease the sails and kicker slightly.

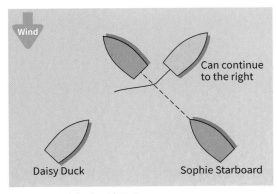

Carry on and duck with Daisy

2. Tacking Underneath
Tacking underneath keeps your options open and enables you to carry on sailing in clean wind (to the left) as, after all, Sophie may be coming across for a reason (starboard may be starting to lift). It also gives Summer the option to tack back if she wants.

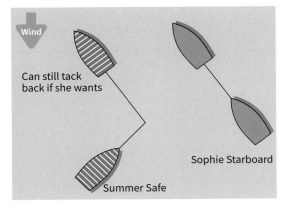

Tack underneath with Summer Safe

3. Leebowing
Leebowing is a good option if you want to defend the left-hand side of the race track.

Leo tacks very close to Sophie (who does not need to take avoiding action until Leo is on a close-hauled course).

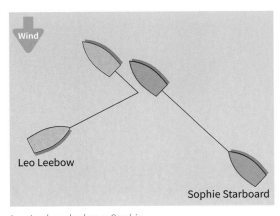

Leo Leebow leebows Sophie

4. Crossing
Crossing is obviously the best option, but make sure you are well clear of the other boat which is

going to let you pass.

Here Daisy is on starboard but, rather than risking Charlotte tacking and leebowing her, she waves her across.

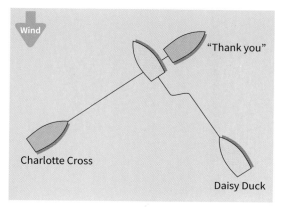

Daisy Duck lets Charlotte cross

Layla is on port and has a good lane (clean wind in the way she is going). She does not want to tack under Sophie Starboard (because she wants to go to the right) and she does not want to duck, or she will be in Charlotte Cross's dirty wind.

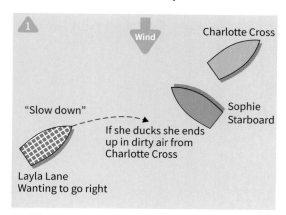

Layla Lane does not want to duck Sophie because she will end up in Charlotte's dirty wind and clean wind is very important

So, to avoid this, Layla slows down (and loses around half a boat length) before accelerating up to full speed to cross close behind Sophie. She can now continue (with minimum loss) the way she

wants to go, still in her lane (also with clear wind).

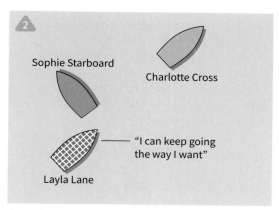

So, Layla Lane slows down, going behind Sophie, but keeping her lane

PLAYING IT SAFE (ADVANCED)

As there are many potential place changes up the first beat (before the start everyone is in equal first place), it pays to have a prudent approach. Keep your head out of the boat and see which side of the race track is winning. If you are not on that side, why not? And can you do something about it?

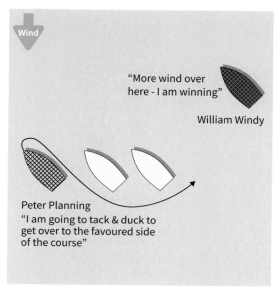

Peter Planning shows it often pays to take an early loss for a bigger gain later

There is a much higher chance of incidents up the first beat, so it pays to stay out of trouble. Remember, when telling someone they can cross, "Go", and "No", can sound very similar! Just shouting back, "Starboard!" or "Keep going", can be much clearer.

However, unfortunately incidents do sometimes happen (mainly to Daniel): Daniel Danger is an expert in doing penalty turns. The quickest way to do them in most classes of boat is to bear away and gybe first, as it is much easier to keep your speed up (bear away, gybe and head up) than it is to tack, bear away, gybe and head up. Make sure that you have plenty of room to do your turns. You don't want to hit another boat whilst doing them and have to do another set!

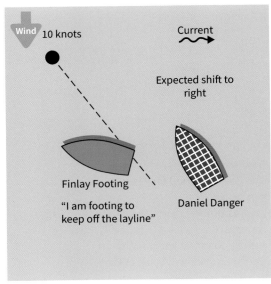

Finlay Footing is footing to stay off the layline and, therefore, he will gain the most advantage from the shift

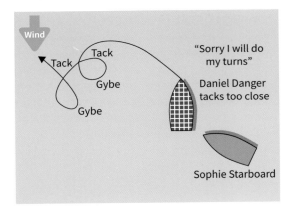

Daniel Danger doing his turns

However, if you cause damage in an incident, you have to retire even if you were the right of way boat. So, don't hit another boat just to prove a point.

One of the key ideas is to keep your options open. This means that, if the wind becomes shifty or becomes stronger, you can take advantage of it; or, if there is an unexpected change (the wind becomes lighter), you are not vulnerable.

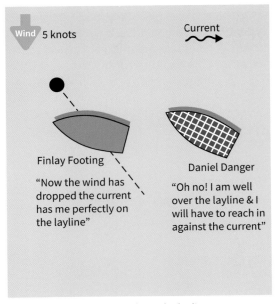

Finlay Footing is now exactly on the layline

BASIC TACKING (BEGINNER)

The goal of a good tack is to maximise your gain to windward. This is not the same as completing the tack as quickly as possible (although this may be necessary sometimes) or coming out of the tack as fast as possible. For more details see chapter 2 in *Coach Yourself to Win* (Boat Handling).

Here Terry Tacker demonstrates three different types of tack:

1. A Good Tack

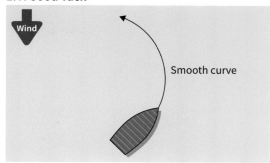

Terry Tacker does a good tack, maximising progress to windward

2. A Fast Tack

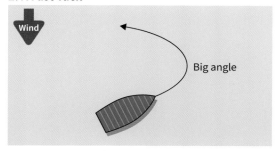

Terry Tacker does a fast tack, where he comes out of the tack fast

3. A Quick Tack

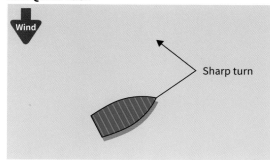

Terry Tacker does a quick tack, tacking as quickly as possible

You can control your speed of tacking to make sure that you end up where you want to be. For example, on (not over or under) the layline or on / off another boat, by speeding up or slowing down the turn.

When you're just tacking to make it around the course as quickly as possible you always simply want to do a 'good' tack. If you then wish to get across to the other side of the race course, you would then foot.

It is extremely rare that it would pay to do a 'crash' tack (where you turn the corner as quickly as possible) as it will take time to get back up to full speed and you lose ground to windward.

If you are tacking on a shift (onto the lifting tack), the tack may be quicker than normal as you might only have to tack through 80° (assuming a 10° lift). Ideally you tack straight away (so as soon as the sail flaps you go), rather than bearing away on the header before tacking. This is why it pays to have your head out of the boat, so that you know that you can tack as soon as a shift comes in, rather than having to check you can cross, etc.

If there is a slight lift as you tack, you may want to slow your tack down as otherwise you may come out slightly below the line you wanted to.

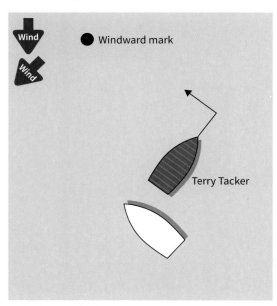

With a big windshift, Terry is going to be over the layline, so tacks as soon as possible

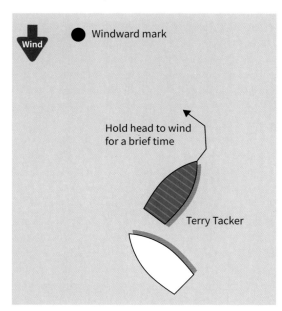

Terry tacks under the layline so, if there is another shift, he can take advantage of it

TACKING TO LOOSE COVER (INTERMEDIATE)

You may want to stay with a particular boat, for example, if the left-hand side of the beat is paying (you are making gains) or you expect it to gain. You don't want to separate from the boat or boats completely, but you stick to the side you expect to gain. This is when you apply a loose cover to stay with your rivals but not forcing them to tack by giving them dirty wind. This way they are likely to keep on going and you are in control.

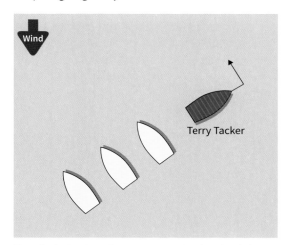

Terry tacks to give a loose cover, protecting the right

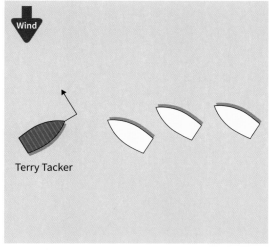

Terry tacks to give a loose cover, protecting the left

TACKING TO TIGHT COVER (ADVANCED)

A tight cover is applied when you must beat a particular boat (you may even need to sail that boat down the fleet) and are not worried about other boats overtaking you both. Here you are positioned directly to windward, giving far more dirty wind. You need to watch them closely to tack as they tack but being wary of dummy tacks! You may find you end up both slowing each other down, especially in boats which lose lots of ground to windward when tacking.

A tight cover can be a way of 'shepherding' a boat or boats. For example, if you want the fleet to go right, you can tight cover on starboard and loose cover on port. This will make them want to go on port (to the right) because this is the only way they have clean air.

To tack in precisely the right place, you may need to speed up or slow down your tack.

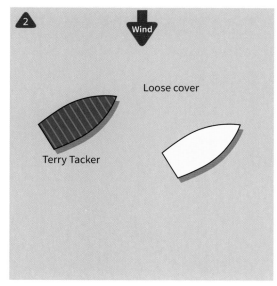

Terry Tacker applies a tight cover on starboard

But when Terry tacks, he applies a loose cover

CHAPTER 6

The Windward Mark

LAYLINES (BEGINNER)

An early layline call makes you vulnerable to a windshift. So, if you are sailing to the corners, perhaps to clear your wind after a bad start, try to avoid the laylines: if you get on them too early and there is a shift then you lose out by either over-standing the mark or having to sail extra distance. Here we can see how Terry Tacker has the advantage over Benjamin and Bethany Corner Bangers.

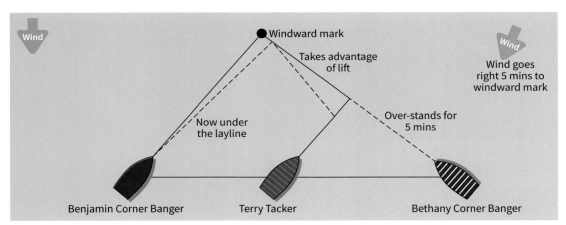

If the wind shifts to the right, Terry Tacker has an advantage over Benjamin and Bethany Corner Bangers because he will gain the most advantage from the shift

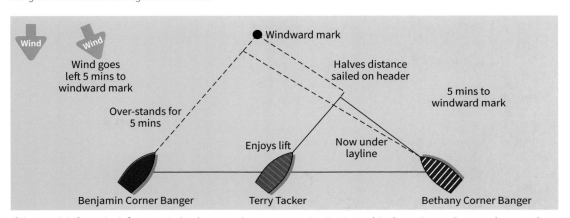

If the wind shifts to the left, Terry Tacker has an advantage over Benjamin and Bethany Corner Bangers because he will gain the most advantage from the shift

It is worth noting that, if there were more shifts to the right than the left, then you would want to sail back to the centre of the course when the wind was in its average direction (see p28).

When you get close to the laylines, there are lots of places to be won and lost just like any other part of the course where boats come close together.

OTHER BOATS (INTERMEDIATE)

Getting on the layline early (giving you a 'long layline') will rarely pay but, when you get on the layline, you want to ensure that you get it right and, in a perfect world, other boats get it wrong! If the course is offset (you spend more time on one tack than the other), then you want to do the 'long' tack first (the one which you are going to spend more time on) as this will keep you further from the laylines.

Here Lily Layline, who is an expert on laylines, bears away as Daisy ducks behind her making Daisy think that she has further to sail to the layline than she does. She then heads back up having gained significantly on Daisy.

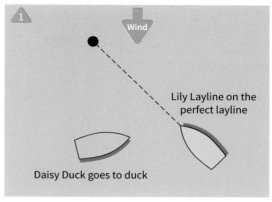

Lily Layline on the perfect layline

Daisy Duck goes to duck

Lily is on the layline and Daisy goes to duck (bear away to pass behind her)

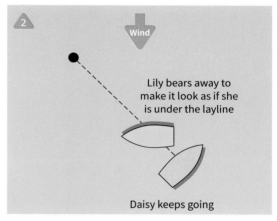

Lily bears away to make it look as if she is under the layline

Daisy keeps going

Lily bears away to make it look as if she is under the layline even though she is not

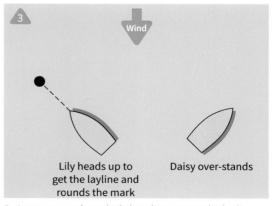

Lily heads up to get the layline and rounds the mark

Daisy over-stands

Daisy over-stands and Lily heads up to get the layline correct

Lily can also force Daniel Danger into a very dangerous position, underneath the layline and unable to tack, by sailing a bit lower and faster and then heading up after Daniel tacks. Here Daniel is in big trouble and he will most likely have to gybe round and look for a gap in the line of boats on the starboard layline.

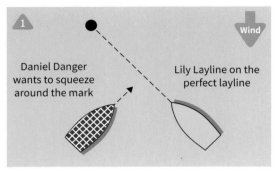

Lily is on the perfect layline

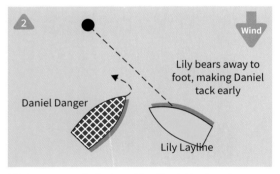

Lily bears away to foot, making Daniel tack early

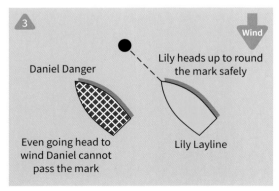

Lily heads up to round the mark, but Daniel cannot pass the mark so he is in lots of trouble!

Poor old Daniel is not having a great time. He once again tries to get around the windward mark (whilst Lily is sailing into the distance) and he tacks inside three boat lengths of the mark. The boats who are on the layline have to luff up above close-hauled and quite rightly protest Daniel.

If he had avoided impeding anyone, Daniel would have had to bear away behind the line of boats on starboard on the layline.

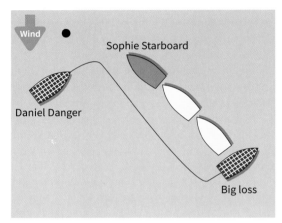

Daniel has to bear away behind the starboard tack boats on the layline because he is the keep clear boat

What Daniel should have done is to have ducked Lily and carried on and then tacked above the layline without infringing anyone like Sarah Safe.

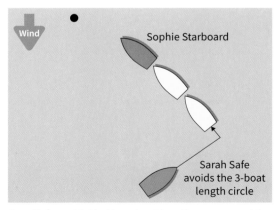

Sara Safe avoids the three-boat length zone around the mark and tacks above the layline so she will definitely be able to make it around the mark

However, a lot of boats will play it slightly safe and over-stand the layline a bit so, if you hit the layline too early, you may well end up over-standing a great deal.

Finally, when choosing your layline, remember that you can, if necessary, pinch up to (but not beyond) head to wind to shoot the mark. This is a very useful skill to have in the tool box as Poppy Pinching has.

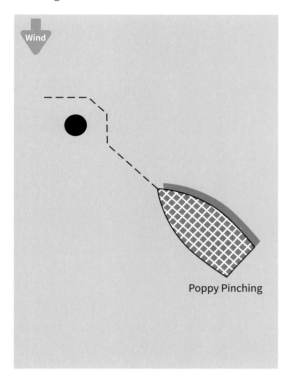

Poppy Pinching shoots head to wind around the mark

STARBOARD ROUNDINGS (ADVANCED)

Rare, but certainly not unheard of, is rounding the windward mark to starboard. This is probably one of the reasons there is often confusion with the rules. *Rules in Practice* by Bryan Willis is a highly recommended read and, just like this book, should always be in your regatta kit bag!

Just like any other windward mark you can rarely approach on port tack unless you are well clear of other boats like Tilley Traffic.

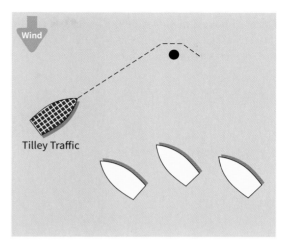

Tilley Traffic approaches with speed on the port layline (making for an easy spinnaker hoist for the downwind leg)

The safest option is to approach on the starboard layline, like Sophie Starboard. Here, if you are approaching on port tack, you need to be careful that you do not duck like Daniel Danger and end up the wrong side of the mark. If you are on the layline and duck a boat, then you are no longer on the layline.

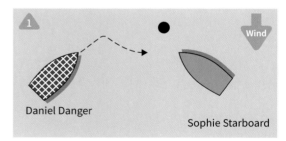

Daniel is on the port layline, but ducks behind Sophie so he is now under the layline

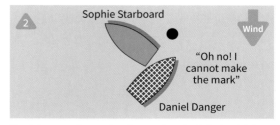

Daniel can no longer lay the mark so he is in trouble!

Better to have a plan like Peter Planning either to tack (and tack back as soon as possible) or just to slow down but hold your course.

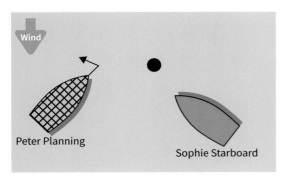

Peter Planning can tack and then tack back as soon as Sophie does

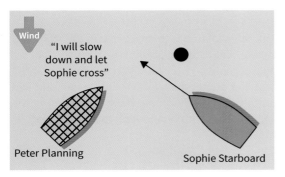

Or Peter can slow down and let Sophie cross

It is very important that you keep concentrating after the windward mark, after all you are on port when many of the fleet who are approaching the windward mark may be on starboard and some may have over-stood the layline. You want to make sure you have a clean lane going downwind.

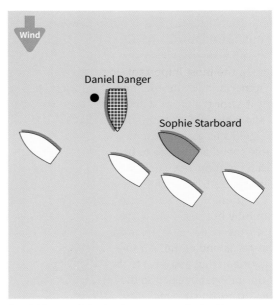

Daniel Danger is in the danger zone – he is either on port tack or windward boat – either way he is the give way boat

If there is a lot of traffic and you have no choice but to come in from the left-hand side of the course then avoiding the other boats like Tilley Traffic is probably your best option. This way you lose a couple of boat lengths early on but avoid the mess at the mark.

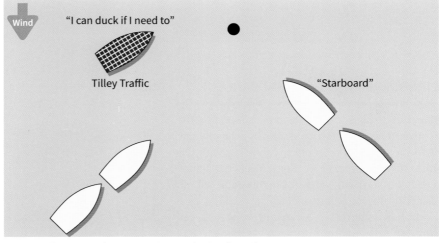

Tilley Traffic approaches above the port layline for safety

CHAPTER 7

Tight Reaching

TIGHT REACHING BASICS (BEGINNER)

One of the most important decisions to make is whether to hoist the kite and, if so, when! If you get it wrong and hoist too early, then you can make a big loss. Get it right and expect to make a significant gain on the fleet as there can be a large speed advantage to be flying the kite when other boats are not. For more details on rig set-up see chapter 5 in *Coach Yourself to Win*.

You must also consider the current very carefully because, when your angle changes, so does the effect of the current. Once again, the danger is ending up too low for the mark. This may mean that you have to drop the kite to make it up and beat back up to the mark or, worse still, end up putting in a tack on a reaching leg.

Many regattas will have a spacer mark before the downwind leg. This means you have a short tight reach to separate the fleet and avoid carnage at the windward mark with boats going downwind meeting those who are still going upwind towards the windward mark. This is especially important for large fleets (perhaps sailing a sausage or inner loop) or very fast boats like twin trapeze catamarans. It is therefore important that the rig is set for a tight reach and then adjusted when you go round the spacer mark for the run. If there is a spacer mark, you should not set the rig for the run as soon as you round the windward mark.

DEALING WITH THE CONDITIONS (INTERMEDIATE)

Important information is what is the wind doing? Was it lifting at the windward mark? And if so, do you think it will continue to lift? Or is it now going to start to head? Are you expecting the wind to increase or decrease along the leg?

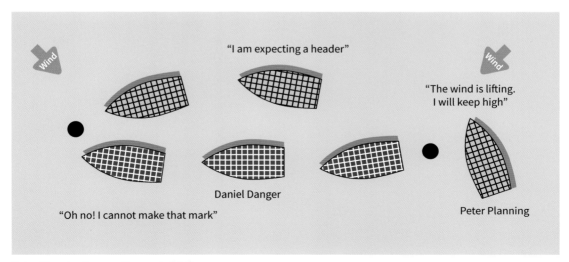

Peter Planning is expecting a windshift

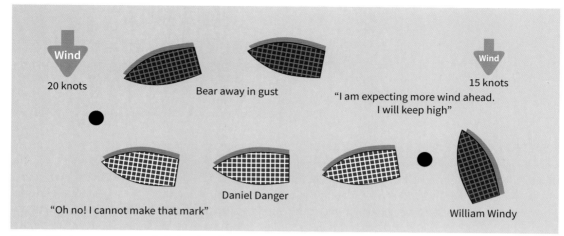

William Windy expects more wind ahead and plans for it

DEALING WITH OTHER BOATS (ADVANCED)

Being rolled to windward on a tight reach is death. Not only will one boat go over you, but probably several, as you get slowed down by all the dirty wind. Because of the tightness of the leg you probably cannot bear away to clear your wind. Even if the mark is a port rounding (so you would have room at the mark), you would think very hard about going low if it would put you in someone's dirty wind.

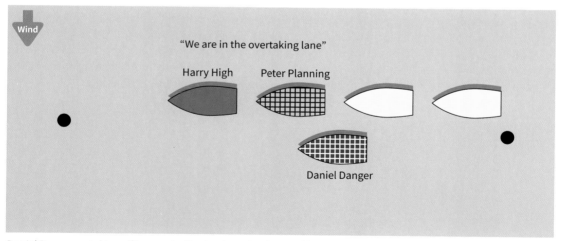

Daniel Danger gets himself in a spot of bother by going low and being overtaken because he is now in dirty wind

BEAM REACHING BASICS (BEGINNER)

In a steadier wind the key thing is to minimise the distance sailed to the mark. However, you must allow for the current, especially if the wind is light compared to the strength of the current. If you simply point at the mark you will sail a lot of extra distance as shown here by Sid Straight Line and Archie Arc.

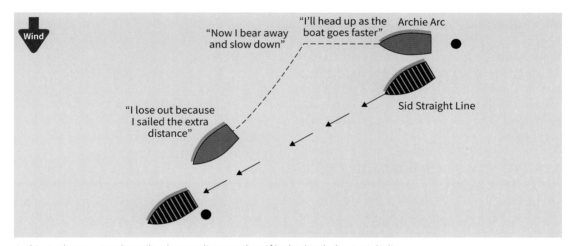

Archie Arc loses out as he sails a longer distance than if he had sailed a straight line

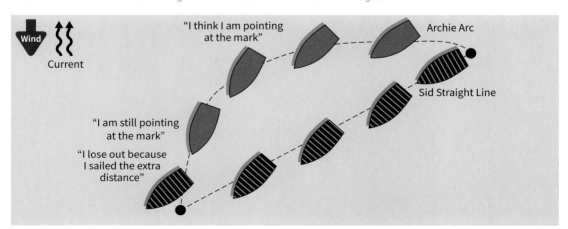

Archie Arc loses out because, despite always pointing towards the mark, the current causes him to sail a longer distance while Sid Straight Line points below the mark and sails directly to it

DEALING WITH THE CONDITIONS (INTERMEDIATE)

In medium winds, where there are gusts, you want to stay in the gusts as long as possible to keep your average speed up. You would bear away in the gusts and then, afterwards, head back up in the lulls.

In planing conditions, you would often want to bear away as far as possible without coming off the plane before coming back up as high as required to stay on the plane. If you spend the whole leg planing when other people are on and off the plane, you will be among the quickest in the fleet.

In strong winds, to avoid a broach, bear away hard as the gust hits so as to take full advantage of it but also to depower it. You can then head back up after the gust passes. If you are struggling to get back to the mark, make sure you hike / trapeze as hard as possible and, if necessary, allow the sails to flap somewhat rather than having the boat heel excessively.

Here, if you followed Georgia Gust closely on a gusty day, you would see her making large movements up and downwind but viewed from a long way above it would look more like a straight line.

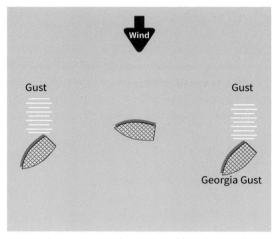

Georgia bears away in the gusts and heads up in the lulls to maximise her time spent in stronger winds

DEALING WITH OTHER BOATS (ADVANCED)

On the beam reach you have the greatest range of course. On a gusty day you could be sailing on anything from a tight reach to a beam reach. The problem is that the fleet tends to act like a flock of sheep – all following each other. You can take advantage of this by keeping away from the fleet.

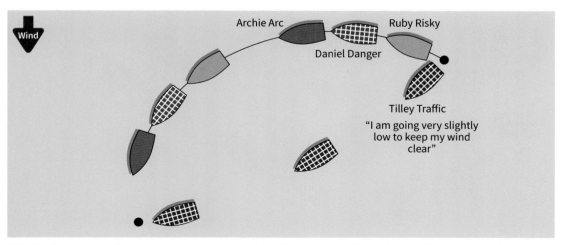

Tilley Traffic separates from the other boats and overtakes them because it is easier to sail fast when you have more space to surf the waves the way you want (clean wind and clean waves!)

BROAD REACHING BASICS (BEGINNER)

Don't be tempted to relax on this leg of the course (just because physically it may be easier than beating or sailing a tighter reach). Just like on any other leg, you need to know whether to prioritise shifts or pressure, but on a broad reach it is often pressure that is the most important thing – it opens the door to performance.

You are unlikely to be overpowered on a broad reach unless it is survival conditions. More often the problem is that you end up high of the mark after you have headed up to increase your speed and you are then unable to bear away back down to the mark without a huge drop in speed.

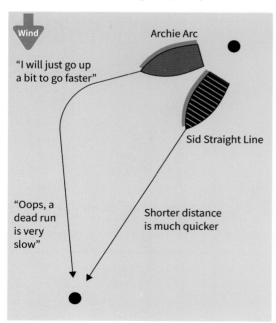

Archie Arc sails a big curve downwind and loses out to Sid Straight Line because Sid sails less distance

You can, of course, see the wind (or rather its effect) on the water, and indeed on other boats, so you should be able to see what is happening and react to it or even predict what is going to happen and be proactive.

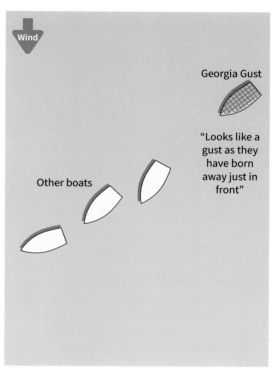

Georgia Gust looks at the effect of the wind on other boats so as to make good decisions

You also need to take a view as to the time frame. Is it worth going up or down for a gust / lull which you can see on the water, but which might never come? Going up will get you into the gust sooner and, once in a gust, bearing away will keep you in it longer.

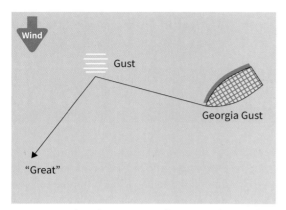

Georgia Gust heads up to get in the gust and gets it first and then has more wind than her rivals

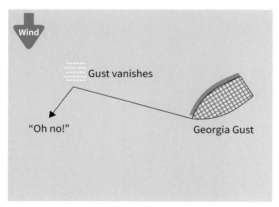

Georgia Gust heads up to get in the gust but it isn't there so she has sailed extra distance unnecessarily

Inland you may expect to steer a lot to maximise the time spent in the gust and to react to changes in wind direction. However, the faster the boat, the less steering you would tend to do in relation to the change. Too much steering could slow you down in a boat which is already planing as opposed to one which has not yet reached full displacement speed.

Even when it is very windy you still need to think about your racing tactics. You should not simply be hanging on and enjoying the ride (or simply surviving), you should be trying to get around the course as quickly as possible!

For more details on soaking low see chapter 5 in *Coach Yourself to Win*.

DEALING WITH THE CONDITIONS (INTERMEDIATE)

It is important to notice if any changes are continuous. For example, is the current gradually increasing or changing direction? This may mean you need to position yourself where there is more favourable current or where you expect there to be more favourable current soon.

If you round the windward mark in slack current, you might expect the current to change inshore first so you would position yourself to take advantage of this (if the benefit of the current is greater than the cost of sailing the extra distance).

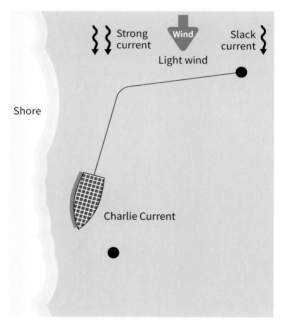

Charlie Current makes the most of the favourable current

DEALING WITH OTHER BOATS (ADVANCED)

When sailing on a broad reach, unlike a run, you cannot simply gybe off to clear your wind (as the extra distance sailed is unlikely to be made up). So, defending is harder. Therefore, you need to make it clear to boats behind that you are not going to let them roll over the top of you.

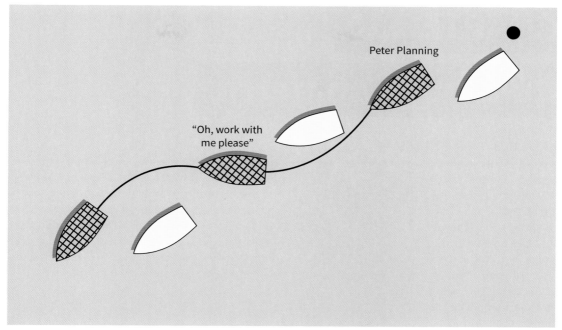

Peter Planning

"Oh, work with me please"

Peter Planning goes up slightly and makes it clear he is going to defend his position

CHAPTER 10
Running Symmetric

BASIC RUNNING (BEGINNER)

Getting the angle downwind is very important and, as conditions change, the fast angle to sail downwind will change also. A good example of a transition would be from non-planing to planing conditions.

When sailing low like Lucas you need to be very careful that the spinnaker does not collapse, as you would then need to head up a lot to refill the spinnaker.

In a single-hander with an unstayed rig, like a Laser, you can sail very effectively by the lee like Lewis Lee. Here the flow of wind goes from the leech to the luff (the mast is now acting as the leech and, due to its stiffness, the flow is very stable). It also gives you good tactical options, allowing you to move around to keep your wind clear and gives you better options to stay surfing on a wave or in pressure without having to put in a gybe.

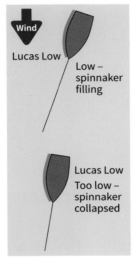

Lucas Low sailing low and too low

Lewis Lee is sailing by the lee

You need to be very careful downwind to keep your wind clear or potentially you could lose a lot of places as, once you get rolled, you are more vulnerable to it happening again. Get your head out of the boat and make sure that you have a clear lane to sail in, just like you would upwind. Pressure is often the most important thing downwind.

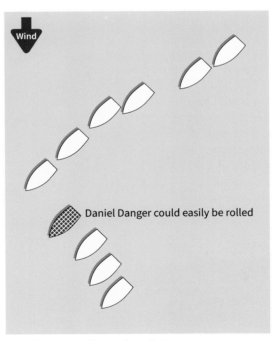

Daniel Danger is likely to be rolled

The aim is to link the pressure like William Windy but also to try to stay in the shifts as well. Although these happen less frequently downwind, in a boat with an unstayed rig you would not have to gybe to stay in the shifts but alternate between broad reaching and sailing by the lee. In a stayed boat you would gybe to stay on the heading tack. You should have an idea of the angles (and also where the pressure is) from the beat.

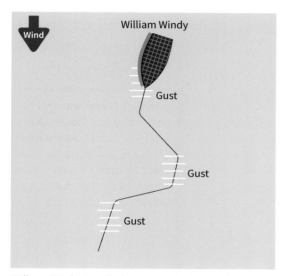

William Windy stays in the pressure downwind

You should also know from the beat whether the course is square and, if not (due to the placement of the buoys or the current), you should keep your options open by sailing the long tack first. You should, of course, always try to avoid as much adverse current as possible and take advantage of any favourable current.

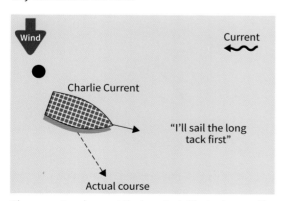

The current makes port the long tack (the tack you will spend longer on than the other tack), so Charlie Current sails that first

DOWNWIND IN WAVES (INTERMEDIATE)

It is not only the wind you need to address: there are also waves. With waves there are basically three transitional stages (as opposed to planing where you either are or you aren't).

1. Not surfing – keep as low as you can without losing speed. In many classes this will be very nearly dead downwind.

2. Marginal surfing – head up or sail by the lee to catch waves.

3. Consistent surfing – you can now pass waves. Just aim for the flat spots as you overtake the waves!

The course may be offset – i.e. you may spend more time on one tack downwind than the other. This may be due to the wind angle or it may be due to the waves. If it is due to the wind angle, then you sail the long tack first just like upwind.

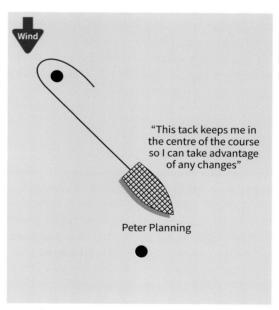

Peter Planning sails the long downwind tack first

However, if it is due to waves, sail the fast tack first. This will allow you to extend and get cleaner wind. If you can surf: surf. There is no guarantee those waves will be there later!

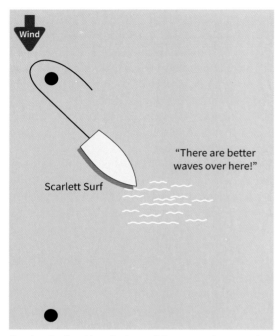

Scarlett Surf making the best of the waves downwind

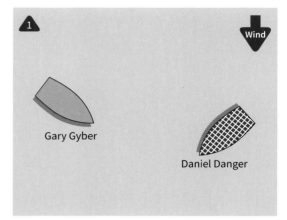

Gary Gyber sails into a position to attack Daniel Danger's wind

In very light winds, where you cannot surf properly, the course may become offset where the waves push you one way, rather like current (but don't actually give you a speed advantage because you cannot surf). Here you would sail the longest tack first.

SAILING AGGRESSIVELY (ADVANCED)

It is still possible to gain places downwind by controlling the other boats, if you are in a position to stop them gybing until the time that you want them to. You turn parallel to the other boat, completely covering it and making it very hard for it to set the spinnaker. You need to plan your attack perfectly, so all the crew in your boat know what they are doing (gybing, soaking or going high) and are prepared. But, if at all possible, don't give any signs about what you are planning, or else the other boats can prepare or change their plans!

Then to close the gap Gary stays directly upwind to give maximum wind shadow. As Daniel slows down, Gary then soaks low to close the gap.

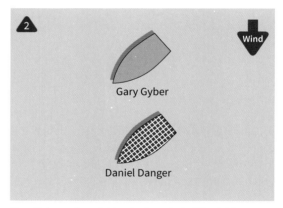

Gary Gyber gybes right onto the wind of Daniel Danger

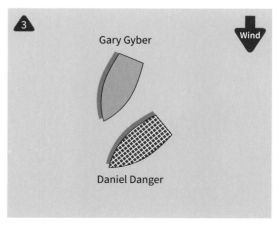

Gary Gyber sails low to give maximum dirty air to Daniel Danger

CHAPTER 11

Running Asymmetric

BASIC RUNNING (BEGINNER)

The key difference between a traditional run and an asymmetric run is the apparent wind: due to the boat travelling faster, the wind appears to come from further forward than the true wind. This means that differences in boatspeed are significant (gusts become very important as the faster we go, the faster we sail through them). Having said this, trapeze boats with large symmetrical kites can also travel very fast downwind and are therefore influenced by apparent wind. For more information see chapter 6 in *Coach Yourself to Win*.

Hitting the right angle downwind is very important in an asymmetric. Go too low, like Lucas Low, and it is easy to get rolled. Go too high, like Harry High, and it is easy to get pinned out so you cannot gybe.

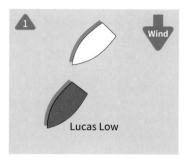

Lucas Low is going low, so closer to the downwind mark, but not as fast as if he pointed higher

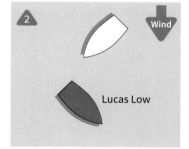

This is fine if he wants to gybe because it is easier to gybe when low

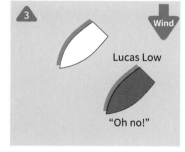

But if he stays on the same gybe, he can easily get rolled because going low is slower than going high

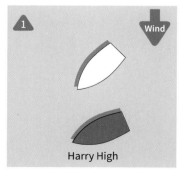

Harry High is going high so further to the downwind mark but sailing faster than if he pointed low

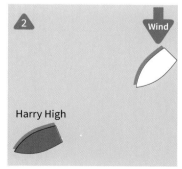

This is fine if the wind is heading or you are sailing into more pressure

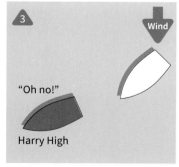

But not good if he wants to gybe because other boats can prevent him from doing so

In strong winds the answer is usually easy – get your weight out as much as possible (through hard hiking / trapezing) and the boat will readily come up to top speed, bringing on plenty of apparent wind, enabling you to go lower. You may even end up going faster and lower than boats which are trying to go low.

When sailing on apparent wind you need to look carefully as to what the wind is going to be doing. You should not only consider the wind you have now but what you are just about to get and what you have the potential to get. The further you think ahead (and therefore plan) the better.

GYBE SET (INTERMEDIATE)

The gybe set is a good option if you wish to protect the right-hand side of the course (maybe there is more wind / better current or the wind is moving right), especially if the leg is quite short.

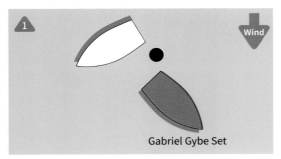

Gabriel Gybe Set

Gabriel gybe sets because she thinks the wind is going right, this maximises the potential gain

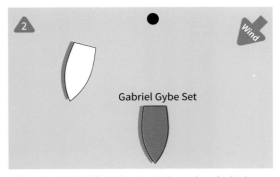

Gabriel Gybe Set

When the wind shifts right, she is clear ahead which consolidates the gain

You must make sure that you are prepared to do this because turning the boat through 180° is a much more difficult manoeuvre than a simple bear away and hoist. The key thing is to keep the speed up and make the turn as smooth as possible. Do not come in on port tack (as this would make it a 270° turn) unless you have no choice. Even if you can tack and sail for one boat length (to get some speed back up) it is much better than trying to do a tack and a gybe around the mark. Be aware of those people sailing upwind (on starboard) on the starboard layline.

SAILING AGGRESSIVELY (ADVANCED)

You want to take each gust down, but you need to be careful of boats going high which could roll you. You want your focus to be on steering accurately for the wind and the waves. You don't want to have all your attention on one boat when you are racing against a whole fleet! So, either go high or gybe off, unless you are comfortably clear of the boats behind.

A good mark rounding (exiting at full speed with the kite pulling as soon as possible) will make your life much easier. Depending on what you want, you can go up high and make it clear that you are not going to let yourself be rolled, or you can gybe off. Don't get in the danger zone like Daniel Danger.

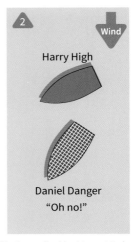

Daniel Danger is in danger of being rolled by Harry High

Peter Planning has a plan to avoid getting caught like Daniel Danger.

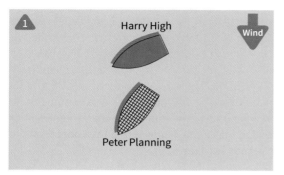

Peter Planning is in danger of being rolled by Harry High

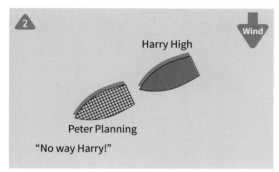

So, Peter Planning also goes high

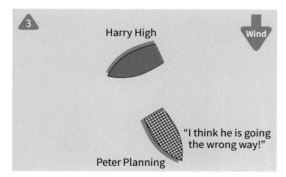

Until he needs to gybe for the mark

To guarantee that you have gained a place, you can simply sail the other boat on until you hit the layline, much like you would upwind. The angle of dirty wind is further forward due to the apparent wind, so consider this when you choose where to gybe.

Peter Planning sails Daniel Danger on until he gets to the layline, so that Peter is definitely ahead

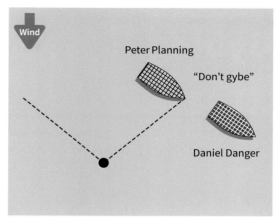

Peter Planning sails Daniel Danger on until he gets to the layline, so that Peter is definitely ahead

Gybing usually slows the boat down considerably. It is often better to slow down and go behind a right of way boat and then to gybe off.

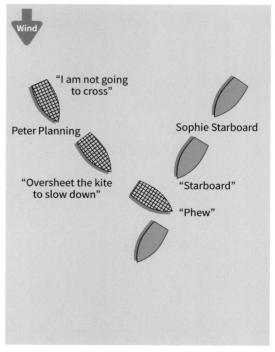

Peter Planning slows down to get down the run faster!

CHAPTER 12

Gybing

AT THE GYBE MARK (BEGINNER)

The best way to get room on a boat is to work your way high then come lower on the final section of the leg. The way to defend against this is to sail (fast) in a straight line to the mark allowing for any current.

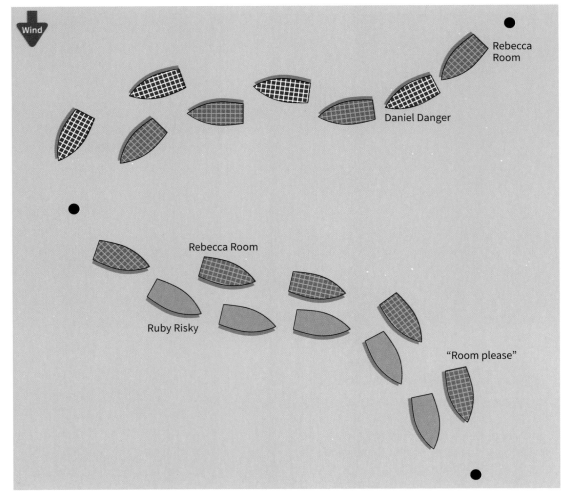

Rebecca Room gets water at the gybe mark by sailing high initially and then low – and getting room at the gybe mark makes it easier to get room at the leeward mark

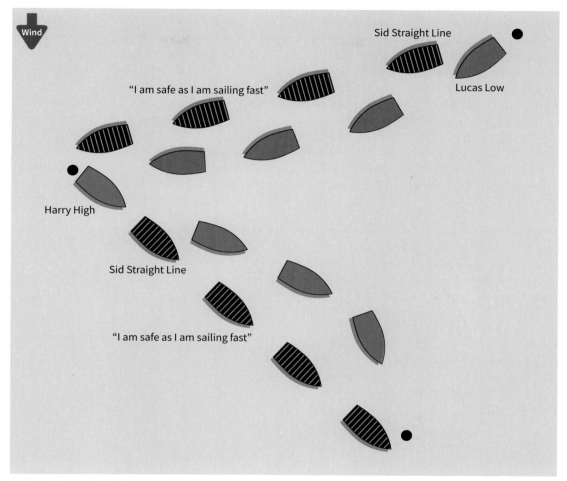

Sid Straight Line defends water at the gybe mark by sailing fast in a straight line and Lucas Low and Harry High don't get room at either mark

When you gybe you need to consider the next leg of the course: you should exit the gybe on the new angle for the next leg.

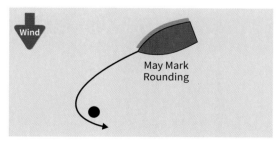

May Mark Rounding goes from a beam reach to a beam reach

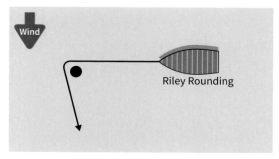

Riley Rounding goes from a tight reach to a broad reach

THE GYBE ITSELF (INTERMEDIATE)

Speed into the gybe really helps with speed out. This is why, tactically, having room to turn is crucial. You are much less likely to have problems when the rig is light than when it is really loaded up: so gybe in the gust, when you are at full speed, not just before the gust hits you! As long as you get these 'big' things right then you can correct any 'little' mistakes that you make (sheeting, steering or bodyweight errors) fairly easily.

- Always turn using a smooth curve, starting when surfing down a wave or in short chop in a 'flat' bit.
- Move your bodyweight as the boat heels to windward and turns, so you are on the new windward side as the sails fill.
- The rudder should be centred (so the rudder and centreboard are in line and not acting as a brake) to accelerate the boat away.

THE ANGLE (ADVANCED)

The faster your boat, the bigger the angle you turn through when you gybe on a dead downwind leg. In other words, if you are sailing mainly on apparent wind, then you will perhaps go through 90° when you gybe (a similar angle to tacking); but, if you are in true wind, you will want to avoid altering course as much as possible, as you would simply be sailing extra distance.

The windier it is the smaller the angle you turn through when run-to-run gybing as you will be sailing lower.

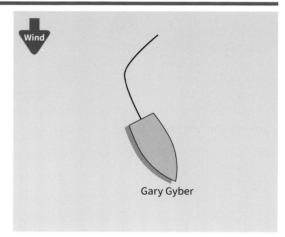

Gybing angle for a medium boat (e.g. single-trapeze monohull)

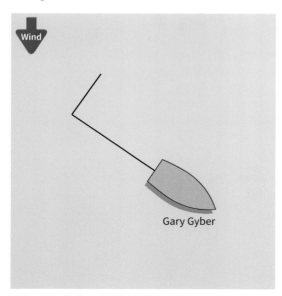

Gybing angle for a fast boat (e.g. twin-trapeze skiff or catamaran)

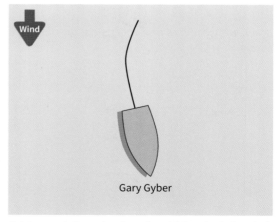

Gybing angle for a slow boat (e.g. hiking single-hander)

BASIC LEEWARD MARK ROUNDING (BEGINNER)

A good leeward mark rounding is essential to set yourself up for the next beat. The golden rule is: in wide and out tight. This means that you can tack when you want or, if you want to keep going, then you can do so in clear air. The aim is to pass the mark at full speed on a close-hauled course so, if you took a picture and edited it to remove the mark, you could not tell the boat had just rounded a mark.

The amount of space required obviously depends on the wind strength and waves (the windier and wavier it is, the more space that you need to do a good rounding) and different classes of boat will perform differently. However, a smooth rounding, using minimum rudder, will work well in most boats as a sharp turn tends to lose all speed.

Remember practice makes permanent. On your own, practise rounding a leeward mark until the drill becomes second nature and you no longer have to think about it, leaving you free to get your head out of the boat to consider your tactical options for the next beat. In boats with a spinnaker, timing is even more important, as it can be very slow trying to sail upwind with the spinnaker!

LEEWARD MARK ROUNDING WITH OTHER BOATS (INTERMEDIATE)

In the absence of other boats, you will approach the mark at full pace – as if you were doing a time trial around the race course. However, the presence of other boats around you may limit your options.

If you do a poor rounding like Samuel Sloppy you have no clear lane and the only way to get clean wind would be to tack off. This is especially damaging in light winds.

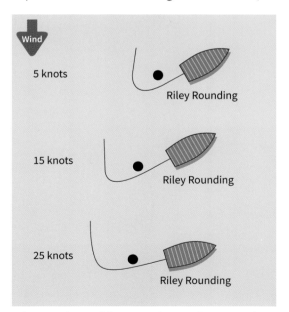

Riley Rounding in different wind strengths: you need to think ahead: doing a strong wind rounding is slow but trying to do a light wind rounding in strong winds may result in a capsize which is even slower!

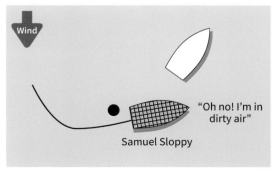

Samuel Sloppy does a poor mark rounding

If you wish to tack off, or the boat in front has sailed high around the mark, then you may need to pinch up (sail close to the wind) in order to ensure you can tack / keep your wind clean.

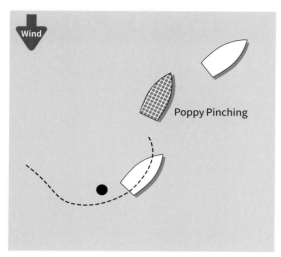

Poppy Pinching can tack off if she wants

The racing line would be a line you would take in the absence of other boats (if you were doing a time trial or a handicap race with no other boats close to you).

You must, of course, allow for the current. Charlie Current would be the outside boat at the mark if he had not allowed for the current perfectly.

Before you get to the mark you should have considered your plan for the next beat, so you can execute it easily. Here Peter Planning knows that he wants to go left, and he has several options as to when to tack. He will go at his earliest opportunity but will wait for a lane if other boats tack first. If he simply needed to sail on, then a good rounding and good speed would be enough.

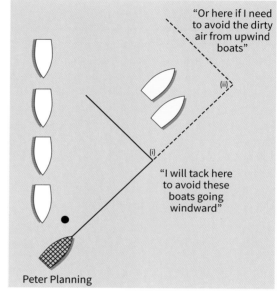

Peter Planning knows what he wants to do and he keeps his options open

Daniel Danger has mark room but cannot take advantage of this

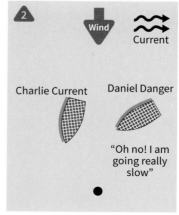

Because Daniel Danger has to sail into the current

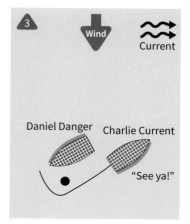

Charlie Current has judged the current perfectly, and rounds ahead

Sometimes the best mark rounding may be achieved by slowing down. It rarely pays to sail around a group of boats. The better option is usually to slow down to ensure a good mark rounding. This can be achieved through rapid steering – heading up, bearing away, heading up, bearing away, etc. – to sail a greater distance.

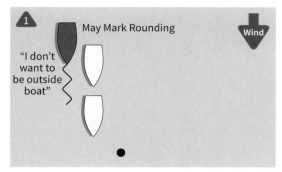

May Mark Rounding is in danger of being the outside boat round the mark so she has a plan

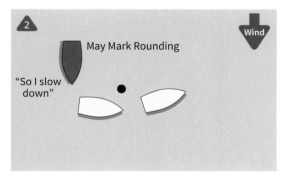

So she slows down to avoid a bad position

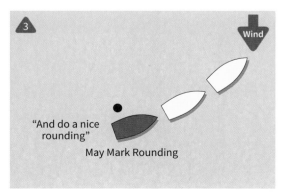

And does a nice rounding with speed and clean air

GIVING OR TAKING ROOM AT THE LEEWARD MARK (ADVANCED)

At a leeward mark you are entitled to room to make a seamanlike rounding: that is the minimum amount of room required to sail to and go around the mark. If you take enough room for a racing rounding (i.e. going excessively wide to begin with) you could end up in the protest room. Likewise, you should not allow someone to take more room than is required.

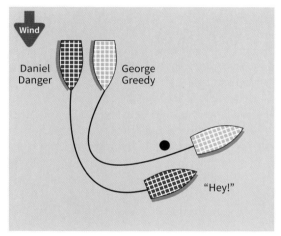

George Greedy takes more room than he is entitled to which breaks the rules

The amount of space required means that actually the boat giving room is in control and therefore should also be able to make a good mark rounding.

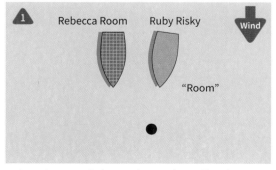

Ruby Risky is entitled to mark room but will make a poor rounding

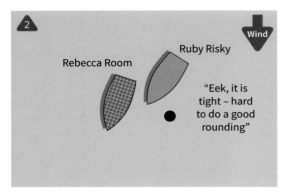

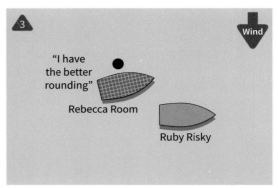

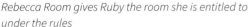

Rebecca Room gives Ruby the room she is entitled to under the rules

So Ruby Risky goes wide out of the mark and Rebecca Room can round tighter to the mark

Of course, if there is the option of not having to give room, this is often preferable. (Although you wouldn't want to lose lots of ground downwind just to stop one boat rounding inside you or risk trying to break the overlap and failing.)

Here thinking ahead really counts. Maybe 80% of the downwind leg is about speed, but near the marks you need to be making decisions, not having decisions made for you.

By luffing (heading up) then bearing away just before the mark room zone you can break the overlap as Oliver Overlap does. The current mark room zone is three hull lengths (this does not include rudder, spinnaker pole etc.) although class rules or sailing instructions can change this.

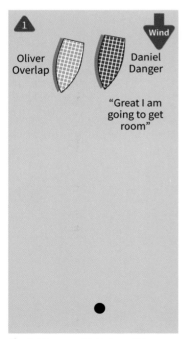

Daniel Danger thinks he will have an overlap and get mark room

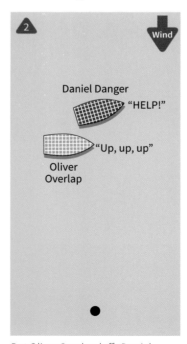

But Oliver Overlap luffs Daniel

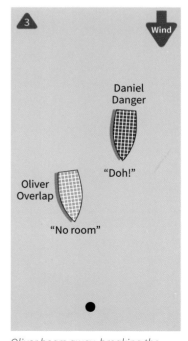

Oliver bears away, breaking the overlap: no room for Daniel

However, a right of way boat (as opposed to one who is simply entitled to room) can make a racing rounding. So, when Riley Rounding is on starboard, she can keep sailing to the point of a racing rounding before gybing and she must be given enough room to gybe (remember the boom has to come across!!!).

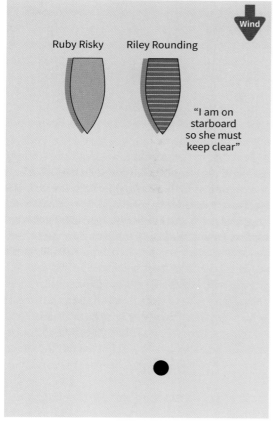

Riley Rounding has right of way: on starboard and to leeward

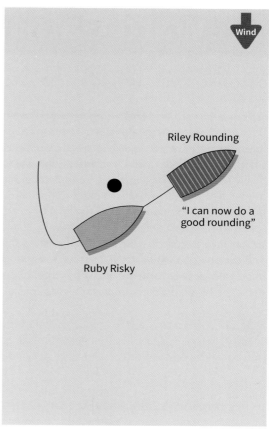

So, Riley Rounding is entitled to do a racing rounding

CHAPTER 14
Leeward Gates

CHOOSING WHICH MARK TO ROUND (BEGINNER)

Due to the extremely tight nature of modern racing it is often necessary to have a leeward gate rather than a single mark to avoid the carnage that would result in everyone trying to go round the same mark. This is especially true of modern asymmetric boats which plane downwind.

Just like a start or finish line, there will usually be a bias to the gate because, with changing wind and current, it is extremely hard to set the marks absolutely square to the wind. The further apart these marks are the more important any bias is.

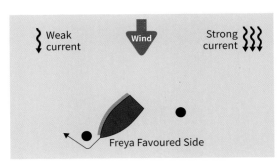

The gate is biased, but Freya Favoured Side chooses the more downwind mark to get to the favoured side of the course for the upwind leg

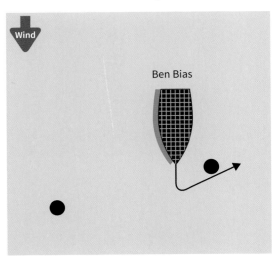

The gate is biased – Ben Bias chooses the closest gate because this means he sails less distance

However, you may choose your gate on the basis of which way you want to go up the next beat, especially in a boat which loses a lot of speed when tacking.

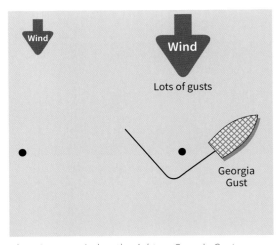

There is more wind on the right, so Georgia Gust chooses the mark closest to the gusts

Or it may be a case of trying to do a good rounding and, therefore, choosing the gate which has the least traffic around it. Not only will it make it easier for you to do a good mark rounding (without having to slow down if you don't have room or are having to defend your position) but it is likely to give you more options up the next beat.

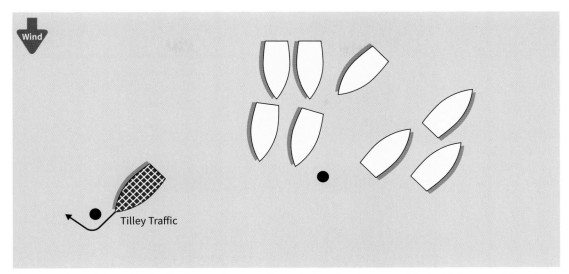

The gate is biased, but Tilley Traffic chooses the more downwind mark to keep out of the traffic because this makes it easier to do a good rounding and have more options upwind

Your approach will, of course, depend upon the proximity of other boats. When going round the starboard gate (looking upwind), well clear of the boats behind, you may choose to come from the left (looking upwind) (on port) to make it easier to do a good mark rounding.

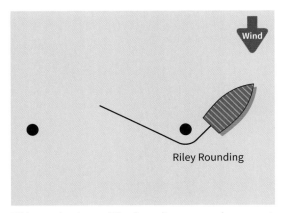

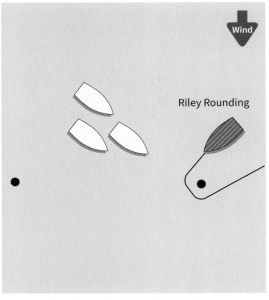

With no other boats, Riley Rounding approaches on port to make it easier to do a good rounding

But with other boats close by, Riley Rounding comes in from the right, on starboard, and gybes round the mark so there is no chance she has to give anyone room

However, if you are with other boats, you may choose to come from the right (looking upwind) so you are coming in as the inside boat on starboard and won't risk having to give someone room.

If you are going for the port gate (looking upwind) then, if you are well clear, you could simply come in from the right (looking upwind) on starboard because this gives you a good mark rounding.

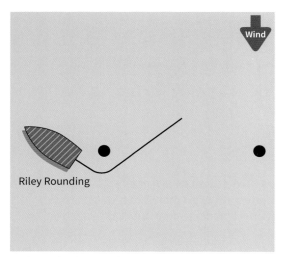

With no other boats, Riley Rounding approaches on starboard to make it easier to do a good rounding

But if other boats are close to you, not only do you risk having to give room at the mark, but you could also be sailing through a large area of dirty air. It's better to come in from the left (looking upwind) on port. But remember that, since you are on port, you are the give way boat until the mark room zone (three hull lengths normally).

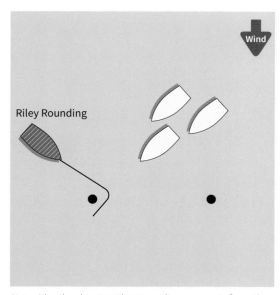

But with other boats, Riley Rounding comes in from the left, on port, and gybes round with mark room

ROUNDING WITH OTHER BOATS (INTERMEDIATE)

Sailing the shortest distance and being the inside boat at the favoured gate is vital and can save sailing a lot of extra distance.

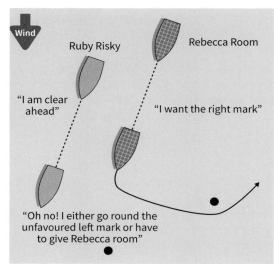

Rebecca Room holds Ruby Risky out (stopping Ruby gybing) until Rebecca is ready to gybe for the mark

If you are not going to be the inside boat round the favoured mark, consider your options.

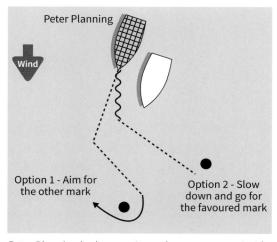

Peter Planning looks at options when you are not inside boat

- Slow down to get inside at the mark but behind with May Mark Rounding. This may mean an early spinnaker drop as soon as you are inside three boat lengths.
- Sail fast and go around the outside if you want to foot left with Finlay Footing. This is more likely to be a viable option in strong winds if you can plane off underneath slower moving boats.
- Go for the other mark if you want to avoid the other boats with Tilley Traffic. You will need to make this decision early because, if you are nearly at the busy mark, it might be a long sail to the other mark.

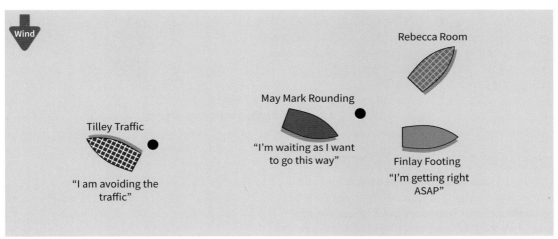

Tilley Traffic, May Mark Rounding, Finlay Footing and Rebecca Room take different approaches to the leeward gate

You also need to consider the tide, not only going into the most favourable / avoiding the most adverse current, but if the current is across the course then this too will influence your choice of gates.

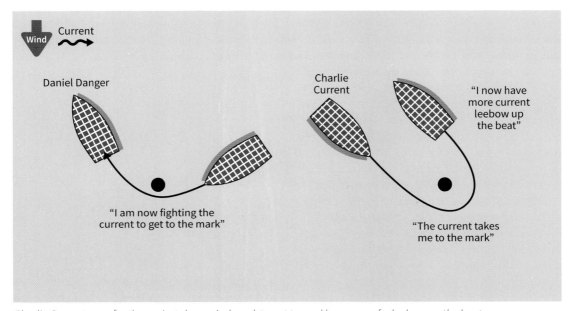

Charlie Current goes for the easiest downwind mark to get to, and has more of a leebow on the beat

Once again, you can break the overlap at the last moment if things are tight, like Oliver Overlap.

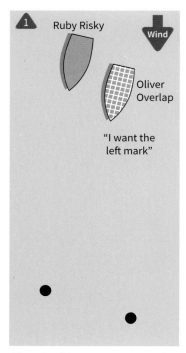

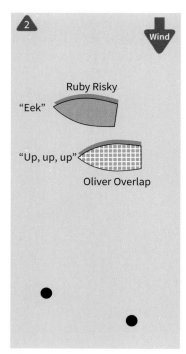

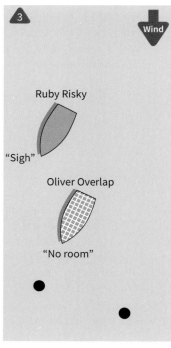

Oliver Overlap wants to go round the left-hand mark, but Ruby Risky has an overlap

Oliver Overlap luffs Ruby Risky

When Oliver Overlap bears away, he has broken the overlap and Ruby is not entitled to mark room

Having rounded the marks, in order to make the most of the shifts you must also consider the traffic, as sailing through the fleet in confused wind and water (and the possibility of collision) can be dangerous and may be worse than sailing on the wrong tack.

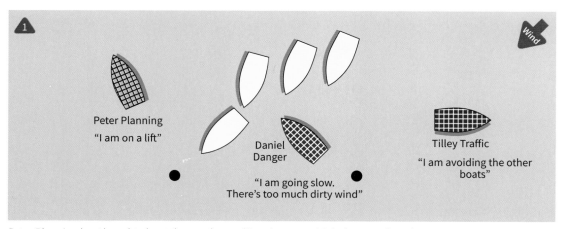

Peter Planning has thought about the next leg and is going to avoid the boats still on the run

Peter Planning ends up in a very strong position because he thought ahead

SAILING AGGRESSIVELY (ADVANCED)

Remember the rules for rounding a mark apply at three boat lengths.

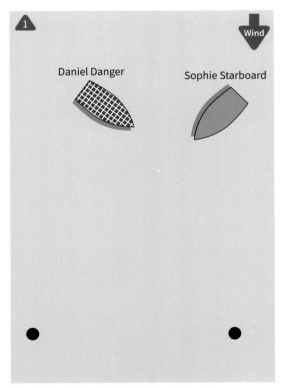

Outside the mark room zone, Daniel Danger loses out to Sophie Starboard

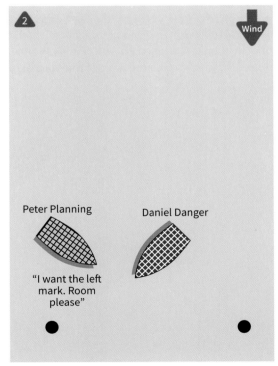

But inside the three boat length zone, Daniel Danger (on starboard) loses out to Peter Planning who, although on port, is entitled to room at the mark

THE DIFFERENCE BETWEEN THE FIRST & SECOND BEAT (BEGINNER)

The main difference between the second beat and the first is that the fleet is more spread out, giving most boats more clean wind. Although this may still be an opportunity to take places, often it is a time to consolidate a good position. With the fleet more spread out you can concentrate more on speed and less on other boats. In other words, set the boat up to go fast rather than be easy to race. See chapter 4 in *Coach Yourself to Win*.

A good example of this was when I was doing some boat tuning work, long straight up rabbit runs, and boat A popped out in front every time. However, we then did some short course windward

leeward racing and boat B won every time. Both crews were of similar ability but one boat was set up for speed whereas the other had an easier set up which made it easier to tack and gybe and accelerate quickly but it had a slower top speed... a classic example of the difference between the first and the second beat. This is an example of changing gear. Boat A was in top gear whereas boat B was in fourth.

It is therefore not surprising that, as soon as the lead boats get a little way ahead and stop 'fighting' with each other, they soon pull clear of the chasing pack. You can still loose cover the chasing pack, but the important thing is to consider the fleet as a whole because it is a consistent series wins regattas.

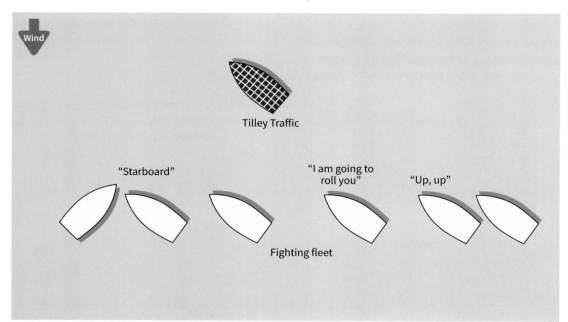

Tilley Traffic is clear and away having avoided other boats

LEVERAGE (INTERMEDIATE)

Generally, the greater the potential gain, the greater the risk. So, like a game of poker, you need to think carefully about how much you are willing to bet on your hand.

To make a gain on the fleet you need to do something different from the pack. Of course, if you are happy with your current position (maybe you are first!), then you may simply want to defend your position (see Chapter 19: Attacking & Defending).

For example, if you close cover someone by tacking on them every time (see Chapter 5: Tacking), you have zero potential gain and maybe a potential loss if the boat you are covering is unwilling to accept a close cover and keeps tacking, slowing you both down. You should not simply fall into the habit of close covering the boat behind just because you don't think you can make any gains.

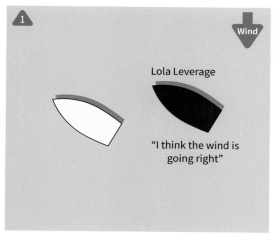

Lola Leverage has a small leverage: she thinks the wind is going right but is not certain

But the wind goes left and Lola loses

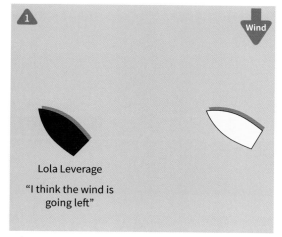

Lola Leverage has a larger leverage and thinks the wind is going left

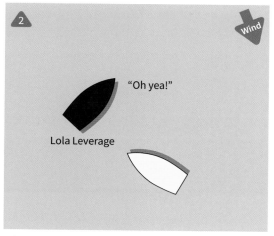

When the wind goes left, Lola increases her leverage

Don't forget that you only actually convert your gain to windward when you tack and cross, so you can 'bank' your winnings!

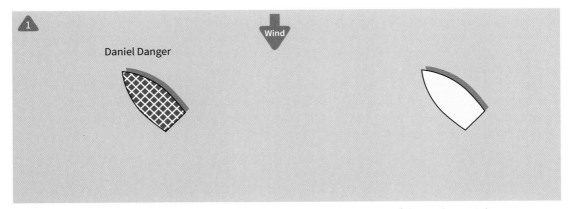

Daniel Danger is hoping the wind is going to go left but is in a dangerous position if the wind goes right

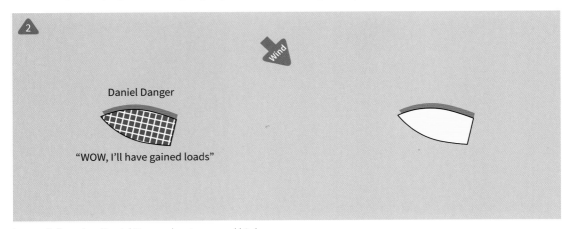

It goes left, and so Daniel Danger has increased his leverage

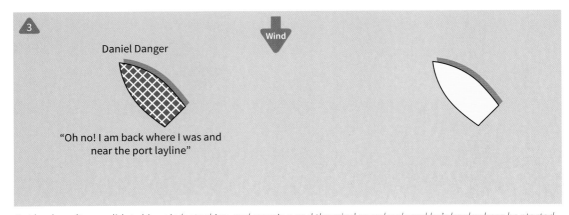

But he doesn't consolidate his gain by tacking and crossing and the wind goes back and he's back where he started

CONTROLLING THE RACE (ADVANCED)

Once you are in a good position, you want to stay there! You need to consider what you would like the boats behind to do. If you are leading the race and the boats near you in the series are further back in the fleet, then you want the places to remain as they are and the race to finish as soon as possible, so you keep some boats between you and them. To extend your lead in the series, you would want to shepherd the fleet to the favoured side of the course.

If, however, you simply want to extend your lead in the race or make it difficult for those boats around you (perhaps they are close to you in the series), allowing other boats to come through, then you make it difficult for the boats close to you to go the favoured side of the course, which will make the race longer and allow more chances for place changes. If a boat is forced to defend its position from boats close to it, then it is unlikely it will be able to sail fast and present a threat to you.

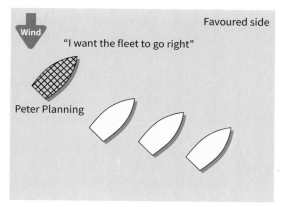

Peter Planning makes it easy for the boats behind to reach the favoured side with a loose cover and, because they have clean wind, they will continue

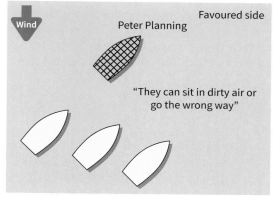

Peter Planning makes it hard for the boats behind to reach the favoured side with a tight cover and, because they have dirty wind, they will be slow

CHAPTER 16

The Final Beat

LONG FINAL BEAT (BEGINNER)

A long final beat (upwind finish) is rare nowadays although some classes still do this, or perhaps a race officer will choose to shorten the course at the windward mark on the final race of the day in fading light or wind (or indeed if the wind is becoming unmanageably too strong) with an offshore wind (as this gives the shortest sail home).

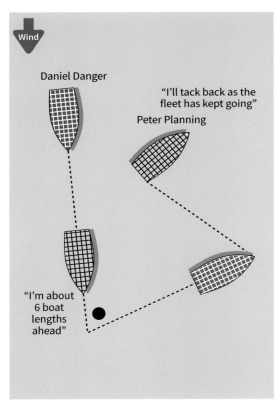

Wind

Daniel Danger

"I'll tack back as the fleet has kept going"

Peter Planning

"I'm about 6 boat lengths ahead"

Peter Planning protects his position at the start of the last beat by tacking twice and applying a loose cover to keep between his rivals and the next mark

By the final beat, the fleet tends to be even more spread out, but this is no time to relax. Place changes can and do happen, and don't underestimate the psychological advantage of finishing a race with a massive lead!

The tactics involved in a long final beat are much the same as the second beat. Loose cover any boats you need to (unless you are consciously trying to sail another boat down the fleet). You should be concentrating on speed and getting across the finish line. Remember your 'position' is not safe until you cross that line and there are no guarantees in sailboat racing. Those boats miles in front of you could break something and you might still be able to overtake them before the finish.

If you are well clear of the boats behind and just want to defend your position, with no particular bias to the beat, then sail for approximately half the distance you are ahead, tack and sail for the other half. Then watch the boats behind. If they tack, go with them. If they don't tack, tack back to loose cover. This means you are not vulnerable to windshifts.

SHORT FINAL BEAT (INTERMEDIATE)

The short final beat usually becomes very much about the finish. You need to consider which end of the finish line and indeed which tack you are going to finish on before you round the leeward mark (see Chapter 17: The Finish).

It is often very hard to gain places, due to the short length of the leg. As there is not much time, it is difficult to get enough leverage. Instead you need to concentrate on not making unnecessary losses, for example, through doing lots of extra tacks or sitting in too much dirty wind.

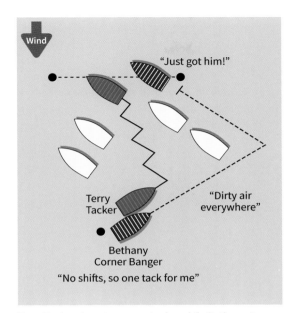

Terry Tacker does too many tacks, while Bethany Corner Banger makes sure she is sailing in clear air

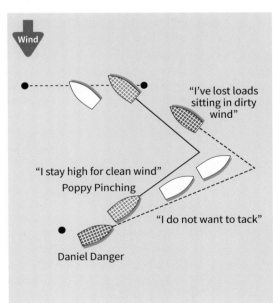

Daniel Danger sails in too much dirty wind, but Poppy Pinching manages to sail higher and has cleaner air

Finally, you must consider that you are trying to get through an upwind gate. Here the current has a huge effect.

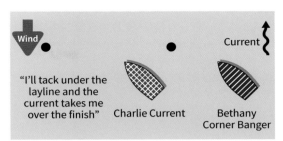

The favourable current is taking you towards the finish, so Charlie Current tacks under the layline but Bethany Corner Banger is over the layline

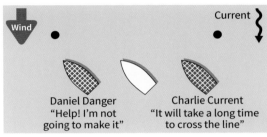

With an adverse current, the opposite is true – Daniel Danger tacked too early and may not make the finish

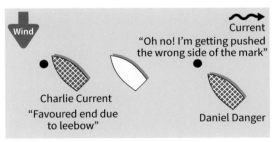

With a cross tide, the end of the line the current is coming from is favoured: you should head for this part

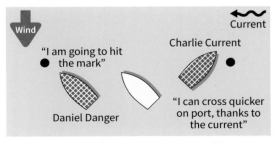

And a cross current from the left may mean it is quicker to cross the finish line on port because of the angle you cross the line on

DEALING WITH OTHER BOATS (ADVANCED)

Keep going! Other sailors may well be tired, and mistakes do happen. You want to be in a position to take advantage of these. Don't simply split tack unless you have nothing to lose.

It is important that you do not allow rival boats to control you. So as someone tacks to cover, you want to time your tack, so you can break away. Make sure they are really tacking (not doing a dummy tack) then aim to complete your tack at the same time. You can then foot to get away from them as quickly as possible.

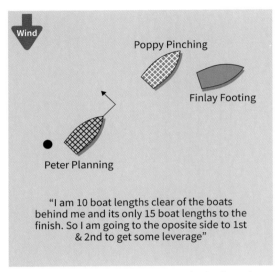

"I am 10 boat lengths clear of the boats behind me and its only 15 boat lengths to the finish. So I am going to the oposite side to 1st & 2nd to get some leverage"

Peter Planning has nothing to lose and splits from the boats ahead because he could gain potentially

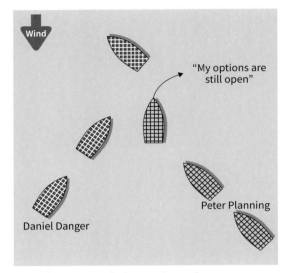

Peter Planning avoids the covering tack

The easiest way to control someone is to sail them to the layline.

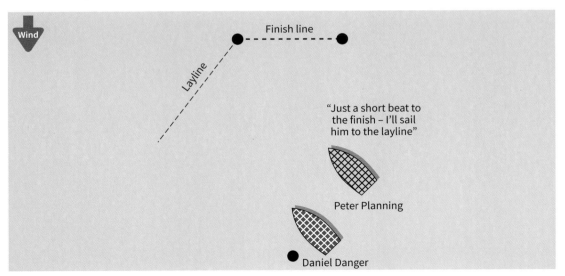

Peter Planning takes control

CHAPTER 17

THE BASICS (BEGINNER)

Always watch out for the shortened course flag!

Don't relax until you have finished. In fact, on a windy day, don't relax until the boat is tied on its trolley, ashore and with the sails down and rolled. It can be very disappointing to have a breakage as a result of a capsize after the racing for the day is finished.

Top tips for finishing (where possible):

- Finish at the favoured end of the line (that which is most downwind for an upwind finish and the most upwind for a downwind finish).
- Finish on the tack which goes most directly across the line. The favoured tack to cross the line may well mean that you need to tack at the favoured end of the line if the line is not square. For example, you may finish at the port end on port.
- In some conditions it may pay to dip (where you go head to wind for an upwind finish or dead downwind for a downwind finish).

You have finished when any part of the boat, in its normal sailing position, crosses the line. If dipping, you need to time it perfectly, usually changing your angle at the last moment so as to directly cross the line. You do not have to completely cross the finish.

Here are some examples of Frederick Finish finishing:

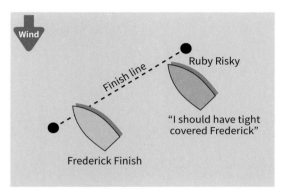

Frederick finishes at the favoured end

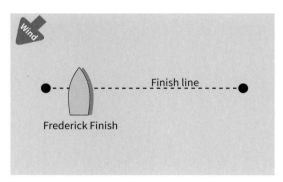

Frederick finishes on the favoured tack, port end

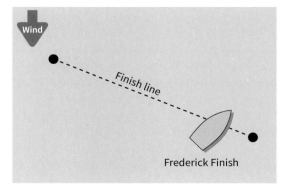

Frederick finishes on the favoured tack, starboard end

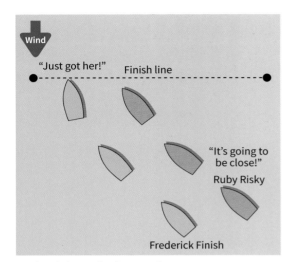

Frederick dips to finish upwind

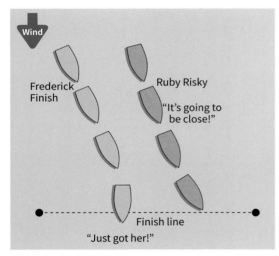

Frederick dips to finish downwind

AFTER THE FINISH (INTERMEDIATE)

When you have finished there are no longer penalties for infringing unless you infringe a boat that is still racing (has yet to finish). Normally you would continue sailing in the way that helps you clear the line as soon as possible. Now is a good time to refuel and rehydrate and have a nice positive debrief. If you have not sailed the correct course, you can still go back (even after the finish) and sail the correct course.

DEALING WITH OTHER BOATS (ADVANCED)

When dealing with other boats you need to keep your options open. As a windward boat with room at the finish, it is usually a good idea to hail to make sure the other boat gives you room. However, in an ideal world, you would be approaching on a layline to the finish (not over the layline).

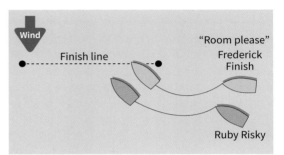

Frederick gets room to finish

A windward boat must keep clear of a leeward boat unless the windward boat has mark room (as above). This means that the leeward boat can go up to head to wind to cross the line.

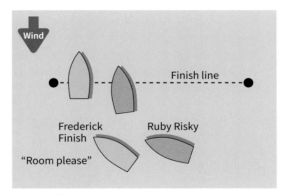

Frederick luffs to finish

However, a leeward boat cannot force a windward boat to tack unless the windward boat has to tack to finish. This means that if the windward boat dips the line you could end up the wrong side of it yourself. However, if he needs to tack, you can ask for room to tack. If he does not give it to you and you have to tack to finish then you can protest.

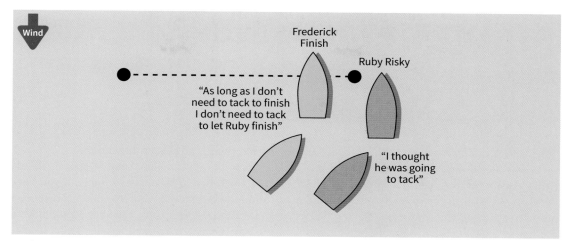

Frederick Finish stitches up Ruby Risky

If you do infringe, you need to take your penalty as soon as possible and re-finish. If you hit a mark, you need to do one gybe and one tack. If you infringe another boat, you need to do two gybes and two tacks. You also need to sail completely to the course side before finishing.

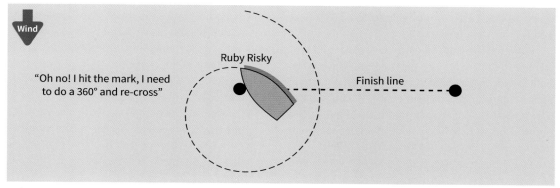

Ruby Risky takes her penalty for hitting the finish mark

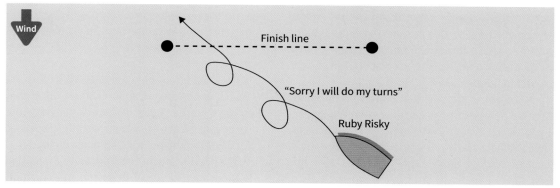

Ruby Risky takes her penalty for hitting another boat

CHAPTER 18

Being Consistent

THE BASICS (BEGINNER)

Being consistent is especially important in big fleets as a small error can result in the loss of many places. You need good decision making, rather than simply seeing what happens – which may work in a smaller fleet if your speed is good but, at a bigger event, you will find the majority of the fleet are fast!

Never get let down by your boatwork. There are usually many signs of wear and tear before items actually fail. When you wash your boat down, check it over thoroughly to see if anything needs to be repaired or replaced.

Plan well ahead so you have done lots of training before your key regattas and have good boatspeed (a fast boat turns you into a tactical genius!) and can rely on your boat-handling skills in pressure situations. You should have already used *Coach Yourself to Win* to establish any goals which need working on well before your key regatta.

You should be aware of the regatta venue and what the key factors are likely to be. Has the venue got strong tide? A good chance of sea breeze? A large area of very high ground which bends the wind or consistently flatter water in one area of the course (maybe due to depth of water)? Being aware of these things will make it easier to take quick decisions in a race as you know what you can expect to happen.

Keep out of trouble. Races are won by sailing fast and pointing the boat in the right direction, not by 'beating' every other boat in the fleet. It really does not help you if you were the right of way boat, but you end up being sunk! If trouble does find you, never give up. One of the best things about sailboat racing is that, however bad the situation

seems, things can always turn around!

Near the end of the regatta you can decide how much risk to take. For example, if you have to win the last race to win the regatta and you are guaranteed second place, then you would have a less conservative strategy (perhaps going further into the favoured side of the course) than if there were lots of boats close on points with you and you had to count the last race (and couldn't afford a bad result).

Key ideas:
- You do not (and should not, due to rule 14) hit another boat to prove that it broke a rule.
- It may not be necessary under the rules to hail (for example, for mark room), but it can help avoid a possible collision which, even if you are in the right, will slow you down.
- Whatever happens, get on with the race (do your turns, protest or do turns and protest). Don't waste concentration that could be making you go faster, in having a shouting match.

However, if there is an incident, here are the key ideas for the protest room:
- You can protest an incident that affected you (you can protest and take a penalty) or one that you witnessed.
- Do not get into a detailed discussion with the boats ashore. Just ask any witness what they saw (so you can judge whether it will help your case) and get the protest form completed using as few words as possible (to make it clear).
- In the hearing, be precise and polite. State what happened and when. Keep the words simple and consistent (I asked for room at three boat

lengths) and listen to the other party's case so you can ask questions. At the end come up with a clear and concise summary (don't just repeat everything you have just said).

HAVE A PLAN (INTERMEDIATE)

Have a plan, have a back-up plan – in fact have two or more!

The key is to stay calm and think rationally. You may have to bite the bullet and change what you want to do but you can never affect what has happened, you can only influence the future. Work out what is the most significant factor (clean air, for example) and work on it. If you are having problems concentrating (maybe due to stress) focus on one thing (the most important – perhaps keeping the boat flat) and then it will be easier to concentrate on others (perhaps steering better).

Planning A Good Start

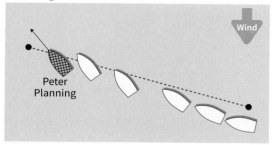

Peter Planning gets a good start at the pin end

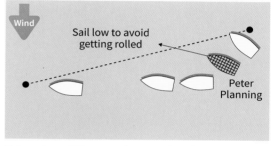

Peter gets an OK start at the committee boat end

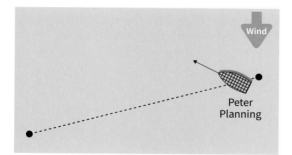

Peter gets a good start at the committee boat end

Peter Planning gets a bad start at the pin end

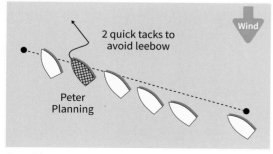

Peter Planning gets an OK start at the pin end

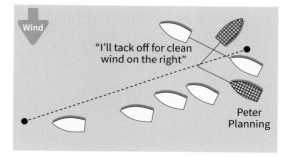

Peter gets a bad start at the committee boat end

Know Your Priorities

Is going the right way more important? Or is clean air? Could this change? For example, if the wind is light, clean air may be most important but, in 25 knots, going the correct way may be crucial. Bear this in mind if the conditions change (for example, a front comes through or a thermal breeze kicks in).

Damage Limitation

If you are unable to avoid sailing in dirty air, then try to limit the damage. If the boat in front is well forward and you are unlikely to be able to sail through the dirty air, consider pinching up to clean your wind.

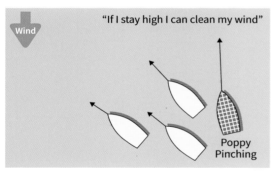

Poppy Pinching avoids slipping further into dirty air

However, if the boat is more to windward, then you need to foot like Finlay to clean your wind as soon as possible.

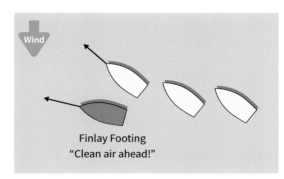

Finlay Footing
"Clean air ahead!"

Finlay Footing gets clean air as soon as possible

If it all goes wrong, don't be tempted to just bang a corner as you can make the situation worse – keep a clear head and keep making the small gains. You would only want to bang a corner (go right to one side of the course) if you really were last and there was nothing to lose! Whatever happens, you NEVER retire (unless of course your boat is so broken you cannot get it over the finish line) as you have no idea what is going to happen later on in the regatta and you don't want to have to count any letters (OCS, DSQ, DNF, RTD, etc.) in your final points!

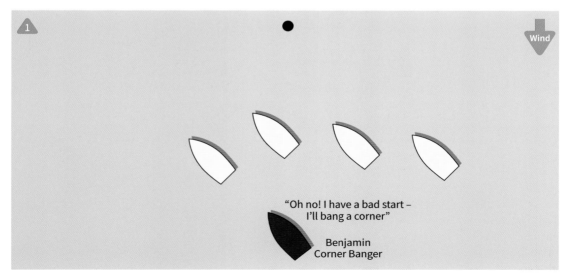

Benjamin Corner Banger decides to do just that: hit the corner (the far side of the course)

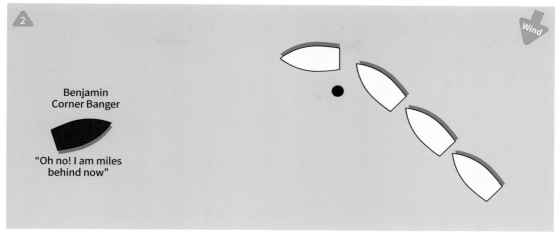

And he ends up even further behind because he went the wrong way

AVOIDING HIGH RISKS (ADVANCED)

Avoid danger areas! Unless you are well clear of all the other boats there are certain 'kill zones' on the race course such as:

Centre Of The Start Line In Light Winds
If you have a bad start in this position, it is hard to get out and get clean wind. Avoid this unless you are confident of a good start and you trust your transits!

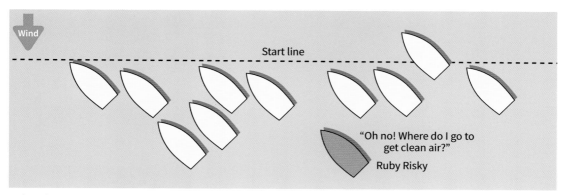

Ruby takes too much risk starting in the centre of a long start line: it is much safer to start towards the favoured end; if you start in the middle, 50% of the fleet are already ahead of you

Hitting The Laylines Too Early
There is usually a slow procession of boats on the layline all sailing a bit high and creating dirty waves for each other up and slowing each other down, especially in light winds. The further away you get from the mark the more likely boats are to have over-stood the mark as they all tack very slightly to windward and give you dirty wind which you cannot avoid since you are on the layline or you have to massively over-stand yourself.

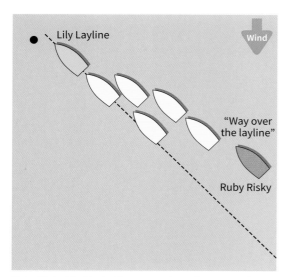

Ruby Risky hits the layline too early and over-stands

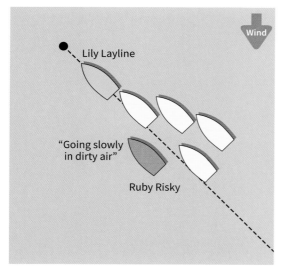

The alternative is to tack earlier and sit in dirty air which is also not a good option!

Arriving at Laylines Too Late

However, if you arrive too late to the layline there may not be a gap for you to tack into. Watch the fleet carefully. If you are just below the layline, duck out early, sail through a gap (there is usually room as long as you are three or more boat lengths from the mark). Just tack as soon as possible to minimise over-stand.

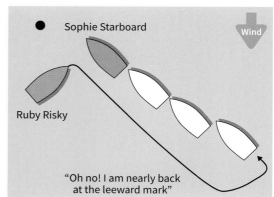

Ruby Risky hits the layline too late and has to duck (bear away behind) lots of boats, losing valuable distance

Tacking Inside The Zone At The Windward Mark

Tacking inside the three hull length circle at the windward mark is a definite no-no as the chance of infringing another boat is high or, if you duck, you could end up having to duck many, many boats before you find a gap.

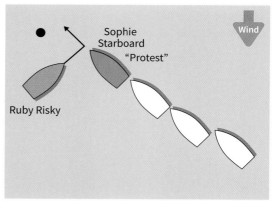

Ruby Risky hits the layline too late and tries to tack in the 3 hull length zone – very risky Ruby!

Complicating Boat Handling

Where you can, make the boat handling as easy as possible to prevent errors, unless there is a large gain to be had. For example, it is much easier (and probably quicker) to round the left-hand leeward gate on starboard and carry on than to come into the right-hand gate on starboard, gybe and drop the kite at the mark, then tack straight after it.

CHAPTER 19

Attacking & Defending

WHEN SHOULD I ATTACK AND DEFEND? (BEGINNER)

It rarely pays to concentrate on beating one boat as the 98 or so are getting away sailing their own race. However, there are key areas of the race course or regatta when this is necessary, so the ability to attack and defend is a vital tool to have in the tool box and one which can be worked on by practising match and team racing skills. Here are some of the key areas:

- At the start – you have no options until you pop out the front (or fall behind). So, you need to concentrate on beating the boats around you.
- When boats meet you will have no choice but to react to the other and whether you cross, tack or duck can have long-term implications for the race.
- When there is a specific boat you have to beat in a race or series. Here you defend the boat to windward by sailing high. This way they do not have the room to roll you and, if they are forced to tack off, you have a clear lane to tack into when you want.

Daniel Danger is not sailing high and is not defending against Poppy

You could also attack boats to leeward by driving over the top of them if you have enough bow forward and space to leeward.

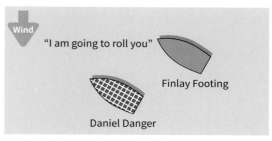

Finlay Footing attacks Daniel by driving over the top of him, giving Daniel dirty wind

In this sequence, Peter Planning uses both footing and pinching to attack the boats around him.

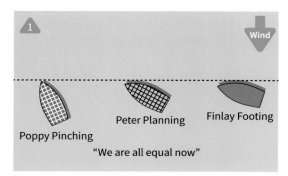

All three boats are level in position

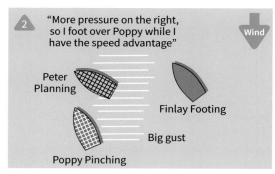

Peter Planning foots off in a gust to attack Poppy's wind

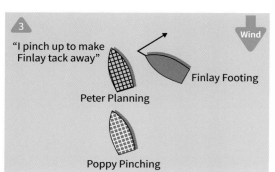

When the gust goes, Peter Planning pinches to make Finlay tack away to avoid a leebow

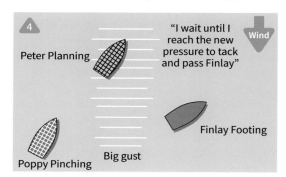

Peter Planning ends up ahead because of his good tactics

SPECIFIC MANOEUVRES UPWIND (INTERMEDIATE)

Leebow

Leo Leebow is the expert at leebowing. This is an important manoeuvre to get right – get it wrong and you get rolled (like Daniel) which means that you not only have to tack back to your original tack (costing you the distance you lose doing two tacks), but you will also be going slower than you were before you did two tacks.

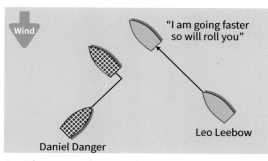

Leo Leebow executes a perfect leebow on Daniel – Daniel now needs to tack off

Daniel Danger tacks too early to try to avoid Leo Leebow but gets rolled instead, meaning he is now in dirty wind

Use the leebow when you want to protect the side of the course. You should not always leebow. There may be times when it is better simply to allow the other boat to cross if you believe they are going the wrong way!

Layline

In order to stop boats tacking in at the layline, bear away to close the gap (three boat lengths). They will either duck you or tack early. Either way you head up like Lily Layline and are safe.

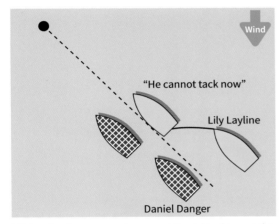

Lily Layline bears away to prevent Daniel tacking on the layline and therefore protects her position

If, however, you are not on the layline, you need to tack as the boat ducks you to stay in control.

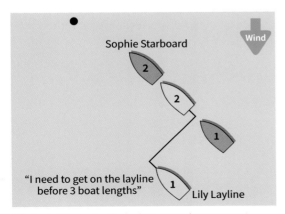

Lily is slightly under the layline, so tacks to get on it while she has the chance

Cover

One of the simplest ways to attack, especially if you are a few boat lengths ahead, is simply to cover. The further you are in front, the less the effect of your wind shadow. You can either slow them down slightly with dirty wind or force them to sail away from the favoured side of the course to maintain clear wind.

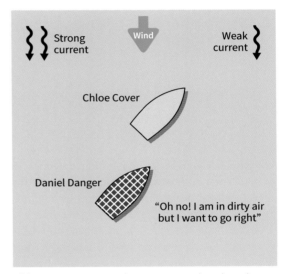

Chloe Cover executes a loose cover, to slow down her rivals

SPECIFIC MANOEUVRES DOWNWIND (ADVANCED)

For many classes of boat, pressure downwind is usually the key factor (for a start, shifts happen less frequently downwind as you are sailing away from them – you are sailing towards them when going upwind!).

On a run it rarely pays to gybe set if there is a spacer mark, as the dirty wind caused by the boats reaching can be seriously bad news unless you are well clear of the pack. So, you would not worry if an attacking boat took this route and you would think twice about defending it unless you were only worried about this one boat or confident this was the way you wanted to go. It would be better to wait until later in the leg to make your move.

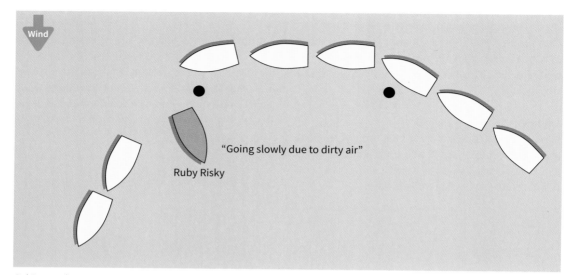

Gybing at the spacer mark, Ruby Risky risks sailing in bad wind and waves caused by the other boats on the reach

The easiest way to pass a boat is often to work high in a lull then drive down hard in the gust. By the time the defender realises, it should be too late, and you are through. Don't go high unless you expect a large change in wind speed, otherwise you may simply end up taking you both high (unless this is what you want).

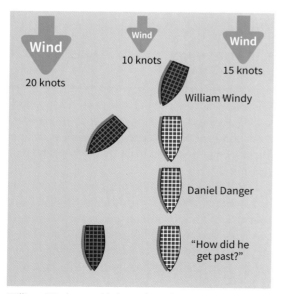

William Windy goes high to where there is more wind and overtakes Daniel

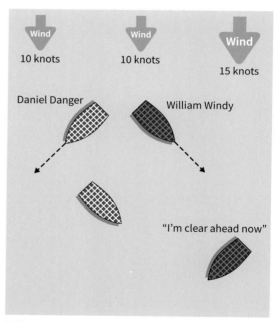

William Windy gybes to get to where there is more wind and overtakes Daniel

You can pass another boat to leeward: this is usually more a case of working the other boat up and then gaining an overlap, as it can be very hard to break through underneath a boat of the same class which is going a similar speed.

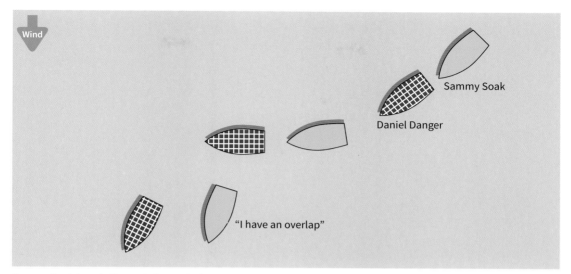

Sammy Soak breaks through downwind

The easiest way to get clear of another boat is to gybe off and sail your own race like Tilley Traffic.

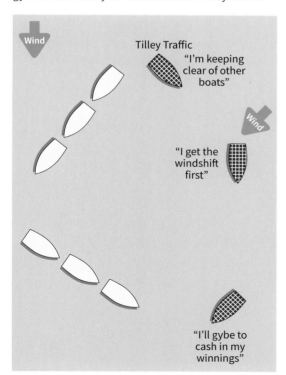

Tilley Traffic gybes off on her own and gets ahead of her rivals

But if you want to attack a specific boat you would want to gybe right in their face. Here you take control of the situation and gybe right when they do… this is why good boat-handling skills are a must. You may need to soak into position like Sammy Soak to do this.

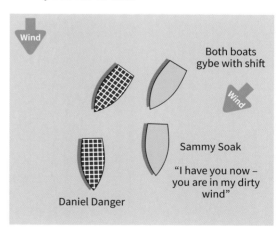

Sammy Soak gybes with Daniel and takes control of him

If someone is trying to gybe on you, you need to make your gybe slick (top crews do not give any signals they are going to gybe). They get the boat going high and up to full speed (breaking any cover as soon as possible).

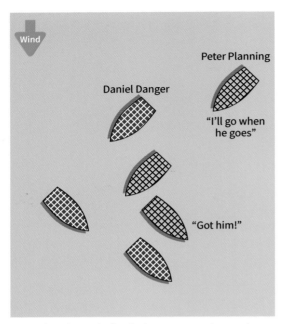

Peter Planning waits for the best opportunity to gybe when to leeward to protect his wind

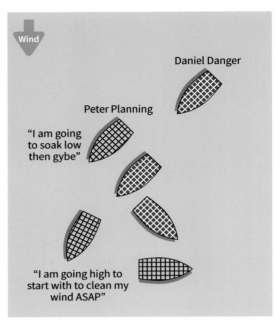

Peter Planning waits for the best opportunity to gybe when to windward to protect his wind

Just like sailing upwind you can use covering to great effect downwind, especially in symmetrical spinnaker boats, forcing them to either sail high, sit in dirty wind or gybe to the unfavoured side of the course.

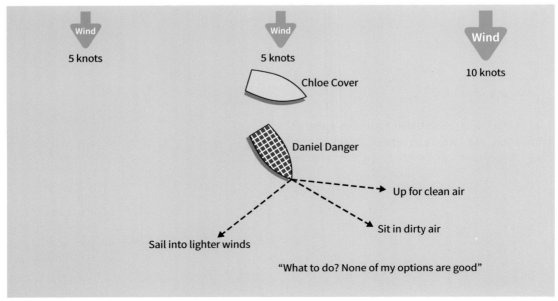

Loose covering downwind with Chloe Cover

FORECASTS (BEGINNER)

Florence Forecast always has a plan and this is based on having the appropriate information available. Sailing is a dynamic sport: there are loads of variables, most of them completely beyond your control (which is part of what makes the sport so exciting but also what can make it rather frustrating at times). One of these key variables is the weather.

Having a good source of weather information is very important. If you always use the same sources, then you will learn if they tend to over- or under-estimate for various venues or perhaps systems tend to come in sooner or later than expected. The more recent a forecast the more accurate it is likely to be.

Here are some good sites:
- www.windguru.cz
- www.metoffice.gov.uk
- www.xcweather.co.uk
- www.windy.com
- www.predictwind.com/

Many sailing venues will also have live weather information, so you can check how closely conditions are reflecting the forecast, for example:
- www.weather-file.com/portland/

Lastly, don't forget you can get up-to-date tidal information. A good site is:
- www.easytide.co.uk

USING THE WEATHER (INTERMEDIATE)

Depressions (a small low pressure feature) crossing a race course can have a profound effect on the race. You will often hear the term 'cyclonic' referred to in shipping forecasts. Here the wind direction is anticlockwise and slightly towards the centre of the low in the northern hemisphere.

Your exact position relative to the path of the depression in the northern hemisphere will affect what happens to you and can be seen by Florence Forecast:

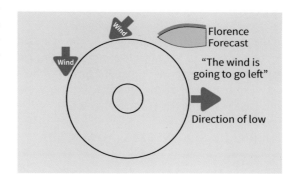

Florence Forecast north of a depression

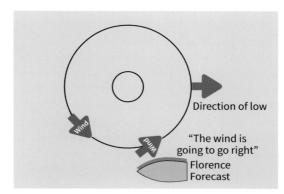

Florence Forecast south of a depression

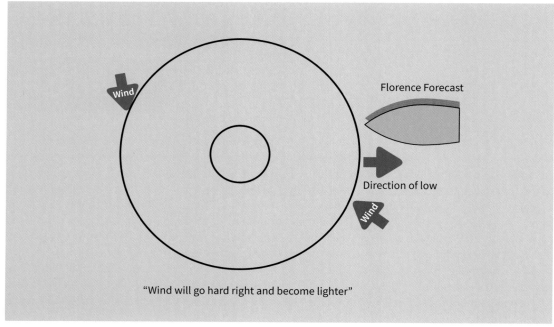

Florence Forecast in the direct path of a depression

In the southern hemisphere things are reversed (the wind is going clockwise in a low pressure).

Low pressures tend to move more quickly than high pressures, high pressures can be very static, especially in the summer time. The flow of wind in a northern hemisphere high pressure is (clockwise) opposite to that of a low pressure, but since they tend to move slowly, they are much less likely to influence you during the course of a race.

THERMAL & SEA BREEZES (ADVANCED)

A thermal breeze is where the land heats up in relation to the water, when the wind is onshore. This may be because, during the course of the day, the sun has warmed the land or it may be a change in water temperature as the tide turns.

In the northern hemisphere, unless the breeze was quite strong to begin with, you would expect the wind to decrease within around four miles of the coastline with the wind slowly veering. If the wind is already to the right, looking offshore, then there may be a slight bend. However, as the wind decreases, pressure across the course will be very different, so staying in pressure is the key to winning races.

A sea breeze starts when the land heats up in relation to the water, when the wind is offshore. There is usually an area of very light or no wind before the sea breeze fully fills in. The right side of the course will nearly always pay when this happens (the sea breeze extends all the way to the shoreline and has burnt off any low mist). The breeze will go right, throughout the afternoon (it would go left in the southern hemisphere).

The diagrams opposite show a south facing coast in the northern hemisphere, but they could easily represent a west facing coast, for example, by rotating them 90 degrees clockwise.

As before, for the southern hemisphere the effects are the reversed.

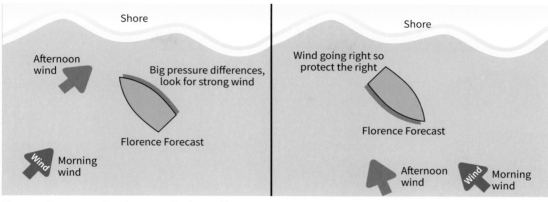

Florence Forecast makes the most of a thermal breeze

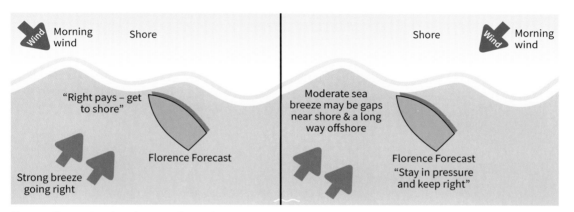

Florence Forecast makes the most of a sea breeze

Index of Boat Names

Archie Arc – Archie sails far more distance than he needs to downwind, sailing a huge arc rather than going straight to the next mark.

Ava Accelerate – Ava is very good at accelerating and she practises, so that she knows just how long it will take her to get up to full speed.

Ben Bias – Ben always goes for the biased end of the line (the one which is the most upwind when starting upwind or finishing downwind, the one most downwind when finishing upwind or starting downwind).

Benjamin & Bethany Corner Bangers Benjamin and Bethany are brother and sister who sail right to the corners of the race course rather than tacking to take advantage of changing conditions.

Brooke Big Fleet – Brooke is an expert at sailing in big fleets and does as many national regattas (across several classes) as he can to gain experience.

Charlie Current – Charlie Current is always keen to maximise his tidal advantage compared to other boats.

Charlotte Cross – Charlotte is slightly ahead and so can cross the boats around her.

Chloe Cover – Chloe uses her wind shadow to slow other boats down.

Daisy Duck – Daisy will duck a starboard boat to carry on the way she wants to go.

Daniel Danger – Daniel allows himself to get into a position where he could easily get rolled.

Finlay Footing – Finlay likes to sail the boat fast and free upwind, bearing the boat away as much as possible without losing velocity made good (VMG) towards the windward mark.

Florence Forecast – Florence always gets a very accurate forecast so that she knows what to expect and can use it to her best advantage on race day.

Frederick Finish – The race is not over until it is over! Frederick is an expert finisher and can often grab those vital few places at the last possible moment.

Freya Favoured Side – Freya always tries to get to the favoured side of the course, considering the big picture.

Gabriel Gybe Set – Gabriel always immediately gybes and sets the spinnaker at the windward mark.

Gary Gyber – Gary is an expert gyber whatever class of boat he is in.

George Greedy – You are only allowed to take so much room to round the mark, George!

Georgia Gust – Georgia takes maximum advantage of the gusts by sailing low in them, then coming back up in the lulls.

Harriet Header – Unfortunately Harriet's wind awareness is not always spot on, so she often sails upwind on a header.

Harry High – Harry sails as high as he can downwind without losing velocity made good (VMG) to the leeward mark. This is good for rolling over boats.

Layla Lane – Layla Lane holds her lane, so she can sail in clean wind the way she wants to go.

Leo Leebow – Leo likes to leebow other boats, forcing them to either tack off or fall behind.

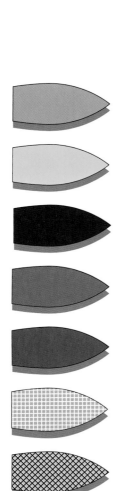

Lewis Lee – Lewis sails a single-hander with an unstayed rig and likes to sail by the lee.

Lily Layline – Lily is an expert at getting the laylines spot on, not arriving too late, too early or too far over or under the layline.

Lola Leverage – Lola uses leverage to pass the fleet but she is a good gambler, only getting lots of leverage when she knows she is going the right way.

Lucas Low – Lucas sails as low as he can downwind without losing velocity made good (VMG) to the leeward mark. This is good for soaking under boats.

May Mark Rounding – May always does a good mark rounding even if it means she has to slow down and follow round behind a boat ahead.

Oliver Overlap – Oliver changes the angle of his boat wherever possible to make and break overlaps. Remember the overlap is on any part of the boat in its normal sailing position (for example, the spinnaker pole or rudder).

Peter Planning – Peter always has a plan and a back-up plan and another back-up plan! Sailing is a very dynamic sport and it always pays to be prepared!

Poppy Pinching – Poppy likes to sail the boat as high (close to the wind) as possible, always trying to head up as much as she can without losing velocity made good (VMG) towards the windward mark.

Rebecca Room – Rebecca is an expert at getting room at the mark and when Rebecca has to give room she gives just enough room for a seamanlike rounding for the inside boat.

Riley Rounding – A good rounding is nice and smooth, so you exit the mark with your 'racing line'. This means that you have a lane in front of you where you can sail without being in dirty wind.

Ruby Risky – Ruby puts herself in areas of the race course which are best avoided!

Sally Shift – Sally is always keen to maximise the gain of an expected big shift.

Sammy Soak – Sammy goes as low as he can downwind without losing velocity made good (VMG).

Samuel Sloppy – Samuel is slow to round the leeward mark (he might get the mainsheet in too slowly for example) which means he has dirty wind.

Sarah Safe – (Summer's sister) Sarah Safe doesn't risk tacking in front of a starboard boat but crosses to stay safe.

Scarlett Surf – Scarlett likes to surf downwind and will always try to get to the best waves.

Sid Straight Line – Sid is very good at taking account of current to ensure he always sails the minimum distance (a straight line) to the next mark of the course.

Sophie Starboard – When Sophie is sailing upwind on starboard, and she sees a port tacker coming across, she just holds her course.

Summer Safe – (Sarah's sister) Summer Safe tacks under a starboard boat to be safe.

Terry Tacker – Terry tacks on the shifts so as to sail on the lifting tack.

Tilley Traffic – Tilley avoids getting too close to other boats by staying away from the pack where possible.

Tyler Transit – Tyler knows exactly where he is on the line as he has a good transit.

William Windy – William is always off to the windiest part of the race course to help his boat go faster.

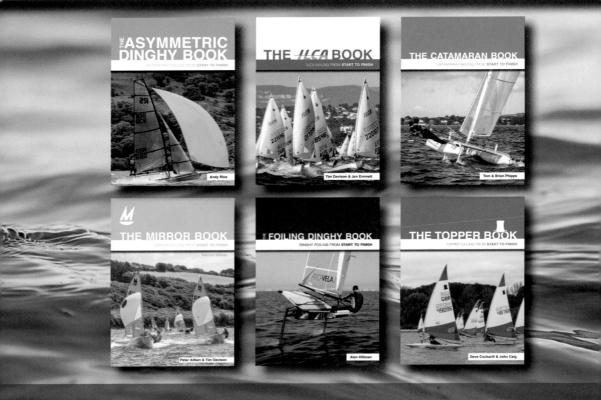

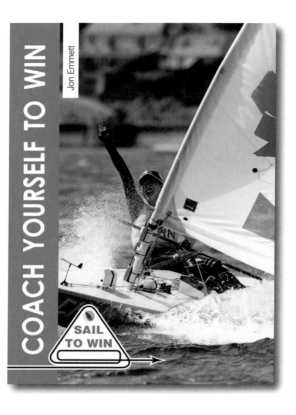

COACH YOURSELF TO WIN

Jon Emmett

SAIL TO WIN

---

sorted before rounding the mark and give yourself a wide enough entrance to the mark to ensure a tight exit. In a perfect world, if a picture were taken just one boat length after the mark, you should not be able to tell that you have just rounded it. So whenever training always finish on a good leeward mark rounding, as it is such an important skill.

A good leeward mark rounding

Summary of Key Ideas

- Keep your wind clear or get into clean wind as soon as possible.
- Stay between the opposition and the next mark (directly upwind on the upwind legs, slightly offset on the downwind legs so as to have clean wind!)
- Protect the favoured side of the course (the side with more wind, better current, etc.)

Advice from Olympic Gold Medallist (Laser class) Paul Goodison

I feel the key to tactics is being able to adapt quickly to changing situations. It is very much about weighing up the risk / reward for each action on the race course. Try to minimise risk and sail conservatively. Generally, the people who make the fewest mistakes win.

It is important to be able to focus on the right thing at the right time. Different weather conditions and fleet positions will require different tactics. I try to keep things as simple as possible, and set myself small goals for different conditions. For example, in shifty conditions, I will always be on the lifted tack, sometimes even if this means that I am in dirty air. In stable conditions, I always make sure that I have clear wind. This may mean that I have to take a small header to clear my lane. I set out these goals for each day, as they are dependent on the conditions and stage of the regatta. It is easy to overcomplicate this area of sailing, generally the people that are winning are just keeping it simple.

CHAPTER 2
Boat Handling

The phrase 'boat handling' refers to any skills that are not directly related to straight line speed. These can often be practised on land where the boat is securely tied to the trolley and you can analyse very carefully what is best to do with your hands and feet with no risk of a capsize.

The important thing is to be able to perform near perfect boat handling manoeuvres under pressure as this gives you lots of tactical options. For example, if you know that you can tack under someone without being rolled, or if you can gybe quickly making it hard for someone to cover you (or easier for you to cover them). You do so many tacks and gybes over the course of a race: if you can make each one just ⅓ boat length better, accumulatively that is a huge distance by the end of the race, and many fewer points at the end of a series.

It is also worth noting that slow speed boat handling skills, like those required pre-start, are very important too. It is not all about achieving rapid acceleration: being able to slow down, hold position and turn without going over a start line are all very important.

Practice

Practice makes perfect so, if you think of all the boat handling that you do during the course of a race, it is obvious that boat handling drills are an essential part of any campaign. When sailing high performance boats for the first time, just being able to get around the race course in the upper wind range can be a real achievement (and it is perhaps worth making sure that your first couple of sails are done in light to medium breezes!).

It is advisable to get your boat handling to a reasonable level before you hitch your boat up to go to your first open meeting as you cannot race effectively if your boat handling is not up to scratch (your strategy and tactics will be compromised if you cannot tack / gybe or get around the marks efficiently).

That old cliché: 'time on the water' is definitely true when it comes to perfecting boat handling, but remember that the more specific and demanding you make the exercises, the greater the potential improvement. By doing a good range of exercises (rather than simply going out and tacking and gybing) it is possible to keep motivation high, and old skills can soon be remembered again with intensive practice. In fact practising boat handling can be an excellent way of developing specific fitness (like doing fast spinnaker hoists and drops).

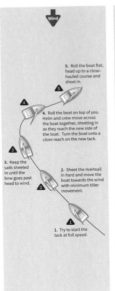

5. Roll the boat flat, head up to a close-hauled course and sheet in.

4. Roll the boat on top of you. Helm and crew move across the boat together, sheeting in as they reach the new side of the boat. Turn the boat onto a close reach on the new tack.

3. Keep the sails sheeted in until the bow goes past head to wind.

2. Sheet the mainsail in hard and move the boat towards the wind with minimum tiller movement.

1. Try to start the tack at full speed.

Best course to sail when tacking

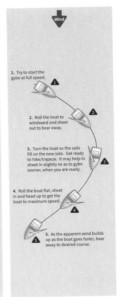

1. Try to start the gybe at full speed.

2. Roll the boat to windward and sheet out to bear away.

3. Turn the boat so the sails fill on the new side. Get ready to hike/trapeze. It may help to sheet in slightly so as to gybe sooner, when you are ready.

4. Roll the boat flat, sheet in and head up to get the boat to maximum speed.

5. As the apparent wind builds up as the boat goes faster, bear away to desired course.

Best course to sail when gybing

TRAINING TO WIN

Jon Emmett

SAIL TO WIN

Stepping Stone Upwind

Sail to the windward mark, and round correctly, sail downwind for 2 boat lengths with sail controls etc. fully adjusted for the downwind and then stop. Then use a Rabbit Start to start again upwind to a new windward mark which you round, sail downwind for 2 boat lengths and then stop. And then repeat with another Rabbit Start and upwind leg to a new windward mark, and so on.

Rabbit start

Rabbit start

This exercise could also be used as a way of progressing to the intended race area rather than towing, or an extended warm-up for getting to a race area, or a way of taking people back to shore and keeping them focused.

Depending upon the venue, it may be extremely important to train on the precise race area to experience the same currents, waves, wind, etc.

Keelboat-Style Steering

Going fast in any boat is about steering the optimum angle to the next mark and so this is a good exercise to focus on steering, separate from the other elements of hiking / trapezing and trimming we discussed earlier. It is all too easy to steer too much or just use all your bodyweight to 'bully' the boat around the course, especially if you are young and fit. So, in this exercise, you sit 'keelboat-style': sitting on the side deck but in reverse, with your legs pointing out (be careful not to drag your feet in the water as it will slow you down). This means that your body weight is fixed and it may even be hard to sheet. This makes good steering suddenly the main focus of your attention.

Sailing keelboat-style

This exercise can be easy or difficult:

Easy	Free sailing keelboat style
Medium	Sail around a course keelboat style
Hard	Racing keelboat style

Advanced Techniques

Holding A Lane

Very often after a start you must hold your lane (continuing on your existing tack at good VMG

Lane Hold

The perfect exercise for this is the Lane Hold: there is a standard 3,2,1, go sequence, but the aim is to get upwind on one tack to level with a buoy, perhaps a 3-minute sail upwind.

Of course, in a real race, after a poor start a boat may be able to get out of the dirty air / leebow effect by footing off (losing some ground to windward but better than sailing in dirty air) or tacking off (again getting into clear air). But the point of this exercise is to learn when you can hold a clear lane and when you can't. The narrower the lane you can hold the better, so pushing it to the limit in training will help you understand this.

without being affected by the boats around you through dirty air / leebow effect etc.) because otherwise you will get bad air or have to sail a lot of extra distance:

- If you try to go low, then you may end up being

Wind

Start line

leebowed by the boat to leeward
- if you try to pinch, someone to windward is likely to roll you and give you dirty air as well
- If you tack you may have to duck more boats and sail a greater distance

In these scenarios it is best to keep going (as fast as you can!) until an opportunity presents itself to do something different.

So, being able to hold your lane is very important. The higher the level of competition the more important this becomes.

Often you may have to hold your lane with

other boats in very close proximity, either because there is an expected shift or there is better current) or because you are not in a position to tack without having to duck a lot of boats and thereby lose a lot of places.

Rabbit Start

It is not always possible to have starting marks or, indeed, someone to monitor the line. A Rabbit Start is a great way of starting an exercise and it also practises your ability to judge speed and distance.

Rabbit Start

The 'Rabbit' sails across the fleet on a close-hauled course (very important they don't reach in at speed as everyone has to be able to judge their approach). Boats then cross at full speed, on a close-hauled course behind the Rabbit.

When everyone has passed behind the Rabbit, the Rabbit tacks (maybe 2 boats past the last boat, but this is wind strength and boat class dependent).

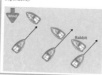

Wind

Rabbit

Rabbit Start

Controlling The Boat

The most important thing is controlling the boat. The advanced exercises overleaf will really push some of you to practise on your own, others in groups. These are time and distance / boat handling exercises. Remember that, even though

you will typically be lining up on starboard tack on a start line, you should also practise on port tack because these are incredibly useful boat handling exercises in their own right.

There are individual exercises and group exercises shown overleaf.

After the start, try to hold your lane for 3 minutes

THE ANDREW SIMPSON
SAILING FOUNDATION

The charity was founded to honour the life and legacy of Andrew 'Bart' Simpson MBE, Olympic Gold & Silver medalist and America's Cup Sailor by using sailing to improve the lives of young people.

Working with sailing providers internationally, the Foundation offers the challenges of a sailing environment to promote health and wellbeing, and to develop personal skills that will improve a young person's ability to succeed in life.